TOFU

Quick & Easy

Revised Edition

Louise Hagler

Book Publishing Company
Summertown, Tennessee

© 2001 Louise Hagler

Printed in Canada by
Book Publishing Company
P.O. Box 99
Summertown, TN 38483

1-888-260-8458
www.bookpubco.com

Food Stylist: Louise Hagler
Photography: Michael Bonnickson,
                        Dan McGarrah Photography
Layout and Design: Warren Jefferson and Michael Cook

On the cover: Spinach Pine Nut Salad, page 37,
Stuffed Jumbo Shells, page 83, Cheesecake, page 118.

ISBN 1-57067-112-5

09 08 07 06 05 04 03 02 01   10 9 8 7 6 5 4 3 2 1

Hagler, Louise.
  Tofu quick & easy / Louise Hagler.
      p. cm.
  Includes index.
  ISBN 1-57067-112-5
  1. Cookery (Tofu) 2. Quick and easy cookery. 3. Vegetarian cookery.
I. Title.
  TX814.5.T63 H34 2001
  641.6'5655--dc21   2001002326

*This book is dedicated to my mother who taught me
to not be afraid to try new and different food.*

Calculations for the nutritional analyses in this book are based on the average number of servings listed with the recipes and the average amount of an ingredient if a
range is called for. Calculations are rounded up to the nearest gram. If two options for
an ingredient are listed, the first one is used. Not included are optional ingredients or
serving suggestions. The amount of calcium in the nutritional analyses in this book are
based on calcium-set tofu, except for those recipes using aseptically packaged tofu.

CONTENTS

A Few Words About Tofu ◆ 4

Breakfast or Brunch ◆ 11

Dips & Spreads ◆ 23

**Salads &
Salad Dressings** ◆ 31

Soups ◆ 57

Main Dishes ◆ 73

Desserts ◆ 117

Index ◆ 135

A Few Words About Tofu

Tofu has only recently found its way into Western supermarkets after having been an Asian staple for over 2,000 years. It is probably the most widely available traditional soyfood, and the most versatile. The question I am most often asked about tofu is "What do I do with it?" The answer is here in these "quick and easy" recipes for today's cook who wants to prepare a delicious meal without spending hours in the kitchen.

Tofu is one of the most versatile and economical foods there is. It is high in complete protein and low in calories, saturated fats, and carbohydrates. This white, mild-flavored, soft block can be transformed into everything from tasty main dishes and side dishes, salads and salad dressings, dips and spreads to sauces, soups, and delectable desserts. Tofu is a culinary chameleon that can assume whatever flavor is added to it.

This revised edition not only updates the original recipes to reflect more current nutritional standards (such as less oil and salt), but also adds more contemporary recipes demonstrating the expanding variety of tofu available on the market. Tofu is now readily available flavored, smoked, or barbecued (great for making quick sandwiches, wraps, or stir-fries), and it is also incorporated into various dairy-free cheeses. The deli department of your natural food store can be a good source of ready-made tofu dishes. Check in the freezer department for more ready-to-cook meals containing tofu.

Tofu's Nutritional Value

Over the last few decades, there have been a substantial number of studies published about the healthful effects of eating soy protein. All the evidence is not in, but the studies so far have shown overwhelmingly positive results.

Coronary artery disease (CAD) is the number-one cause of death in the U.S. In 1999, the FDA authorized the use of health claims about the role of soy protein in reducing the risk of CAD. The FDA concluded that foods containing soy protein included in a diet low in saturated fat and cholesterol may reduce the risk of CAD by lowering blood cholesterol levels. Scientific studies show that at least 25 grams of soy protein daily in the diet are needed to show a significant cholesterol-lowering effect. A food must contain at least 6.25 grams of soy protein per serving in order to qualify for this health claim. A quarter pound of tofu can contain between 8 and 17 grams of protein, depending on its density. Soy protein has also been shown to lower the "bad" (LDL) cholesterol, but leave the "good" (HDL) cholesterol alone. Studies have also shown soy protein to help in the prevention of diabetes, kidney disease, and gallstones.

There are many other health-promoting nutrients in soybeans, including omega-3 fatty acids, iron, and calcium. Some tofu is set with a coagulant made from calcium sulfate (often referred to as calcium-set tofu). This form of calcium is easy for the body to absorb and helps maintain bone density. Tofu that is made this way can contain up to 300 milligrams calcium per quarter pound. The amount of calcium in the nutritional analyses in this book are based on calcium-set tofu.

Soybeans contain natural plant chemicals known as phytochemicals which are believed to help protect the body from disease. The specific phytochemicals in soy, isoflavones, are antioxidants that have been shown to neutralize "free radicals" in the body that are believed to contribute to illness and aging. Isoflavones have also been shown to help protect against some hormone-related cancers, including breast, ovarian, and prostate cancers.

Tofu is a wholesome, complete vegetable protein that is very easy to digest. This makes it a good food for almost everyone, including babies (over 6 months), children, and the elderly. It is an excellent food for people with sensitive stomachs. Its great versatility can add variety to the diets of people who are allergic to milk or eggs, or those who follow strict dietary laws prohibiting dairy products.

The protein in tofu promotes growth as effectively as meat or dairy products. Tofu contains all of the essential amino acids for the body's energy and protein needs. For the nutritional analyses in this book, we used an average profile of 124 grams of regular or medium-firm tofu (a little over ¼ pound) containing 94 calories, 9 grams protein, 5 grams fat, 3 grams carbohydrates, and 250 milligrams calcium. The nutritional content of different types and brands of tofu will vary, so be sure to check the food labels on the package.

Types of Tofu

Regular tofu is made by the traditional method of curdling soymilk, then straining and pressing the curd. Soymilk is made by soaking dried soybeans overnight, grinding them into a paste, adding the paste to boiling water, and cooking for about 20 minutes, then straining. A curdling agent is added to the hot soymilk, and depending on how the curdling process is followed, the curd can result in tofu that is anywhere from soft silken to extra-firm. Most traditional tofu sold in the West is regular or medium-firm, unless otherwise noted on the package. Medium-firm is best for mashing, crumbling, or careful slicing; firm or extra-firm is best for slicing or cubing when you want the tofu to hold its shape. Firmer tofu will also have a higher protein content. Regular tofu is usually refrigerated in a water or vacuum pack and can be found in both natural food stores and supermarkets.

Silken tofu in aseptic packaging is not prepared by the traditional method. Hot soymilk is mixed with a thickener, poured into the packaging, and sealed. It congeals in the package into soft, firm, and extra-firm densities and is not separated into curds and whey. Silken tofu has a more pudding-like or gelled texture than regular tofu, which makes it great for blending into dressings, sauces, and puddings. It does not freeze well, but will last for months unopened on your kitchen shelf. Once it is opened, it should be treated like fresh tofu—stored under water in your refrigerator. This kind of tofu can be found in both natural food stores, supermarkets, and Asian markets.

Snow-dried (or freeze-dried) tofu originated in the mountains of Japan where freeze-drying was found to be a good way to preserve it. Snow-dried tofu has a chewy texture and can be easily rehydrated. Backpackers like this form of tofu because it is a compact, lightweight form of protein that needs no refrigeration and is easy to add to soups, chili, sauces, or stews. Snow-dried tofu is available at natural food stores.

The Care and Handling of Tofu

Really fresh traditional tofu has barely any scent at all. It has a slightly sweet, mild vegetable aroma. If you live near a tofu maker, try some while the curds are still hot for a special treat.

When buying tofu, look for the freshest possible, checking the expiration date on the package. If the tofu is not vacuum packed and sealed, gently rinse it under cold water when you bring it home, then store it covered in cold water in the refrigerator. If you rinse it and change the water every day, it can keep for up to two weeks. If either mold becomes visible, it turns a pinkish color, or it becomes slimy, throw it out. Tofu can still be used if it has a slightly sour smell, but it must be cooked for at least 20 minutes. This can be done by boiling it in water (which changes it to a harder and chewier texture) or by using it in a recipe that calls for at least 20 minutes of cooking or baking time. Slightly sour tofu makes a fine baked cheesecake.

Use only the freshest tofu for recipes that call for no cooking. If you are using fresh tofu in a recipe that does not require cooking, such as a tofu salad, dip, or pie, blanching the tofu first will help the finished products keep longer. Blanching can be done by cutting the block of tofu into quarters and simmering the pieces in boiling water for 10 to 20 minutes. This won't change the texture significantly and will serve to "freshen" and stabilize the tofu.

Any unused portion of an opened package of tofu should be kept in the refrigerator under water, with the water being changed daily to help keep it fresh. Give your tofu the sniff test daily when you change the water. If the tofu you buy smells sour when you open it, or looks pink or bubbly, take it back to your grocer for a replacement and recommend that he keep it at a cooler temperature.

If you want a denser tofu or a drier tofu than you have on hand, remove water from the block by loosely wrapping it in a kitchen towel and placing a weight (like a cutting board) on top for 10 to 20 minutes.

When blending tofu either in a blender or food processor, break or cut up the block into smaller pieces for quicker and more consistent blending. Firmer tofu may need some liquid added to assist the blending. See Useful Kitchen Tools, page 8.

Freezing Tofu

If I can't use my tofu within a few days of opening it, I wrap it up and put it in the freezer to use later. Freezing tofu changes it to a more chewy, meaty consistency, expanding its versatility even more. It makes great Fajitas (page 100) and Barbecue (page 78). It can be frozen right in the package or each block wrapped in plastic, foil, or put in a freezer bag. Frozen tofu seems to holds its shape better in cooking if it is not frozen in water. Before it is used, it must be thawed and carefully squeezed dry. It will resemble a spongy latticework and will soak up marinade and sauces more readily than fresh tofu. When it is frozen, tofu changes color from white to light tan. It takes 6 to 8 hours to defrost frozen tofu at room temperature or overnight in the refrigerator. For fast defrosting, pour boiling water over it in a bowl, use a microwave oven on the defrost setting, or simmer the frozen block in water.

Measuring Tofu

Traditional tofu generally comes in one-pound blocks. A pound of tofu is equal to two cups. A home scale is useful if you need to measure, or try the water displacement method. To measure ½ pound tofu by this method, fill a 4-cup measuring cup to the 3 cup level, then add a piece of tofu or enough slices or cubes to bring the water level up to the 4-cup mark. You will get to where you can estimate pretty easily after weighing or measuring a few times.

Silken tofu in the aseptic packaging comes in approximately 12-ounce packages, which is ¾ pound, or 1½ cups.

Marinating Tofu

Marinades and tofu work together very well. With meats, long marinating is usually done to tenderize a tough cut, as well as add flavor. With tofu, the marinating process is used to add flavor.

A long marinating time is not necessary. Tofu can be marinated for anywhere from a few minutes to overnight in the refrigerator for the flavors to soak in and blend. If the tofu is to be cooked, the cooking will bring out the flavors in the marinade. Marinating should always be done in a glass, stainless steel, or enamel container. A flat pan works best for marinating slices or cubes. Turn the pieces several times or use a bulb baster to suck up and squirt the marinade over the pieces. To avoid the risk of bacterial growth, store marinating tofu in the refrigerator.

Useful Kitchen Tools

There are several kitchen tools that are helpful when cooking with tofu. A food processor and/or a blender are essential. Either one will work well in these recipes, although some food processors will not make as creamy a final product as a blender. Unless you have a high-powered blender, a food processor is more efficient because it will blend all the ingredients at once. A regular household blender may require several batches. To save wear and tear on your blender motor, blend only half a pound of tofu at a time. You can mix all the ingredients for a recipe together in a bowl, then blend one cup at a time in the blender. Stir all your blender batches together in the end. Also, with a blender, you may have to add a little more liquid than the recipe calls for and you may have to coax the blending along, oh so carefully, with a rubber spatula. An electric mixer can be used to blend softer tofu for dips, dressings, and spreads. If you lack these kitchen power tools, the softest tofu can be blended by hand with a wire whip.

Using These Recipes

Tofu is truly a vegetarian fast food. The recipes in this book usually take less than 30 minutes to prepare. In some cases the cooking time will be longer, but in many cases the whole recipe can be ready to eat in 15 minutes or less. Since everyone works at a different pace, the timing will vary from cook to cook. Before you start, be sure to read through a recipe so you will have a clear idea of what the procedure is. A microwave oven can be used to speed up cooking for casseroles that only need to be heated. I have only given conventional oven cooking times because each brand of microwave has a little different power and settings. Since you are familiar with your own type of microwave oven, you will be able to convert the times and settings.

Other Ingredients You May Need

Miso is a traditional soyfood that is cultured and fermented to produce a variety of flavors, colors, and concentrations. It is a salty flavor enhancer with overtones from sweet to savory, like full-bodied, fine wines. A little goes a long way; a serving may be anywhere from a teaspoon to a tablespoon, depending on the type. Traditional unpasteurized miso is a living food with friendly bacteria that can aid digestion, help maintain alkaline blood, and help the body recover from radiation exposure or other pollutants The beneficial enzymes in miso are destroyed by high heat. Traditional miso production can take anywhere from one to three years depending on the type. The lighter-colored miso, usually called sweet or mellow, is milder, less salty, and usually sweeter than the darker-colored ones. Darker-colored miso contains more salt, protein, and essential fatty acids, but offers less of the beneficial bacteria than lighter, sweet, or yellow miso. Traditionally, darker-colored miso is eaten in the cold months and lighter in the warm months. You can find miso in the refrigerator case of your natural foods market or by mail order.

Nutritional yeast is a dried, food-grade yeast. The best tasting nutritional yeast I know of is Saccharomyces cerevisiae. It is the type used by Red Star Vegetarian Support Formula, also known as T-6635+. It is a good source of vitamin B_{12} and is easily digested. Available in both powder and flake form, nutritional yeast contains protein, including all essential amino acids, and six of the B vitamins. With a cheesy, nutty flavor and a golden color derived from its riboflavin content, its flavor lends itself well in spreads, sauces, salad dressings, crackers, breading mixes, on vegetables and popcorn, and in soups and gravies. Store it in a cool, dark place. Nutritional yeast is available usually in bulk at natural food stores or by mail order.

Nonhydrogenated margarine is produced without hydrogenation. Hydrogenation converts liquid oils into hard fats by forcing hydrogen into them, which changes their molecular structure and results in the conversion of unsaturated fats into both trans-fatty acids and saturated fatty acids. These are known to increase the "bad" or LDL cholesterol in the body, which can increase the risk of heart disease. Trans-fatty acids interfere with the critical balance of essential fatty acids in the body. Nonhydrogenated margarine is available in both supermarkets and natural food stores.

Dairy-free or nondairy cheeses are available in many flavors, from cheddar to Parmesan and in many forms from shredded to slices and chunks. Brands will vary in texture and flavor, and their ability to melt, so you might have to try a few to find the ones you like. These are great alternatives to cholesterol-laden dairy cheeses. You can find them in both supermarkets and in natural food stores.

BREAKFAST OR BRUNCH

Apple Kuchen ◆ 13

Boofers ◆ 17

Broccoli Quiche ◆ 18

Bruchettas ◆ 20

Fried Rice with Tofu ◆ 21

Hash Browns ◆ 17

Mexicali Rice Bake ◆ 22

Mushroom Quiche ◆ 19

Mushroom Scrambled Tofu ◆ 15

Scrambled Tofu ◆ 14

Scrambled Tofu Rancheros ◆ 16

Spanish Rice ◆ 22

Whole Grain Pancakes ◆ 12

Whole Grain Pancakes

Yield: 12 (3-inch) pancakes

Use whatever combination of whole grain flours that you like. Below is one example of the possibilities. You may have to add a bit more soymilk depending on how much liquid is absorbed by the grains. This is an easy dry pancake mix to make in bulk at home. Store it in a sealed container in the freezer. Serve the pancakes with maple syrup and Soysage or Tempeh Sticks (from Soyfoods Cookery, *page 138). See photo, page 33.*

Mix together:

½ cup cornmeal
½ cup barley flour
½ cup oat flour
½ cup unbleached wheat flour
½ tablespoon baking powder
½ teaspoon salt

Pour in:

2 to 2½ cups soymilk

Stir with a whip just until blended, then stir in:

½ pound regular tofu, mashed or crumbled

Pour onto a hot oiled griddle using ⅓ cup per pancake, and cook until browned on both sides.

Per Pancake: Calories 97, Total Protein 5 g, Soy Protein 2 g,
Fat 2 g, Carbohydrates 15 g, Fiber 3 g, Calcium 27 mg, Sodium 96 mg

Blueberry Whole Grain Pancakes: Stir in 1 cup fresh or frozen blueberries with the tofu.

Apple Whole Grain Pancakes: Stir in 1 cup grated apple with the tofu.

Apple Kuchen

Yield: 6 servings

Preheat the oven to 375°F.

Blend in a food processor or blender until smooth:
   ½ pound regular tofu
   ⅓ cup sweetener of choice
   ¼ cup unbleached flour
   ½ teaspoon baking powder

Stir in:
   1 cup peeled and chopped apples
   ½ cup chopped walnuts

Spread in an oiled 9-inch pie pan, sprinkle with cinnamon, and bake for 45 to 50 minutes. Cut into 6 wedges and serve hot.

Per Serving: Calories 163, Total Protein 4 g, Soy Protein 3 g,
Fat 8 g, Carbohydrates 19 g, Fiber 1 g, Calcium 113 mg, Sodium 4 mg

Scrambled Tofu

Yield: 3 cups

Try this as a replacement for scrambled eggs.

Heat in a nonstick skillet:

1 tablespoon olive oil

Stir in and sauté until transparent:

1 small onion, chopped
1 small green pepper, chopped
1 to 2 cloves garlic, minced

Stir in:

1 pound soft or regular tofu, crumbled or mashed
2 tablespoons nutritional yeast flakes
1 teaspoon salt
½ teaspoon poultry seasoning
½ teaspoon turmeric
¼ teaspoon freshly ground black pepper

Stir and fry until the tofu starts to brown. Serve with toast, bagels, tortillas, potatoes, or rice.

Per ½ Cup: Calories 92, Total Protein 6 g, Soy Protein 5 g,
Fat 5 g, Carbohydrates 4 g, Fiber 1 g, Calcium 91 mg, Sodium 365 mg

Mushroom Scrambled Tofu

Yield: 3 cups

Heat in a nonstick skillet or wok:

1 tablespoon oil

Stir in:

1 cup sliced mushrooms
½ cup chopped onions, or 1 tablespoon onion powder
1 pound soft or regular tofu, crumbled
1 clove garlic, minced, or ¼ teaspoon garlic powder

When the tofu starts to brown, stir in:

1 tablespoon soy sauce
1 tablespoon chopped fresh parsley

Serve with rice, noodles, or toast.

Per ½ Cup: Calories 87, Total Protein 6 g, Soy Protein 6 g,
Fat 5 g, Carbohydrates 3 g, Fiber 1 g, Calcium 168 mg, Sodium 174 mg

Scrambled Tofu Rancheros

Yield: 3½ cups

Make this colorful breakfast protein as spicy as you like. See photo, page 33.

Heat in a skillet:

1 tablespoon olive oil

Stir in:

1 clove garlic, minced
1 small onion, chopped
½ teaspoon turmeric
1 pound regular tofu, crumbled

Cook and stir for about 5 minutes, then stir in:

1 large tomato, chopped (1½ cups)
2 tablespoons chopped fresh cilantro
1 (4-ounce) can green chiles, chopped and drained
1 teaspoon salt

Stir and cook until the tofu starts to brown. Serve hot with hot corn or wheat tortillas, and pass the salsa.

Per ½ Cup: Calories 85, Total Protein 5 g, Soy Protein 5 g,
Fat 5 g, Carbohydrates 5 g, Fiber 1 g, Calcium 152 mg, Sodium 314 mg

Boofers

Yield: 12 patties

Have ready:

3 cups mashed potatoes from instant or leftovers

Sauté together:

1 tablespoon oil
1 medium onion, chopped

Mix into the potatoes along with:

½ pound regular tofu, crumbled
¼ cup minced parsley
½ teaspoon salt
¼ teaspoon black pepper

Shape into 12 patties ½ inch thick, and brown each side about 4 minutes in:

2 tablespoons oil

Per Patty: Calories 78, Total Protein 2 g, Soy Protein 1 g,
Fat 3 g, Carbohydrates 8 g, Fiber 1 g, Calcium 54 mg, Sodium 93 mg

Hash Browns

Yield: 4 cups

Heat in a nonstick skillet:

2 tablespoons oil

Add:

1 pound frozen Southern-style hash browns or frozen grated or cubed potatoes

Cover a minute, then stir a few times to thaw, and add:

½ cup chopped onion
½ pound soft or regular tofu, crumbled
1 teaspoon salt
¼ teaspoon black pepper

Cover and continue to cook until the potatoes start to brown. Flip to brown the other side. They will not hold together in one piece. Serve hot.

Per ½ Cup: Calories 104, Total Protein 3 g, Soy Protein 2 g,
Fat 5 g, Carbohydrates 16 g, Fiber 1 g, Calcium 34 mg, Sodium 289 mg

Broccoli Quiche

Yield: 8 servings

This is a moist, tender quiche with subtle flavors.

Preheat the oven to 350°F.

Boil in 1 inch of water for 5 minutes then drain:
3 cups broccoli florets, drain

Sauté together:
1 tablespoon olive oil
1 cup chopped onion
3 cloves garlic, minced

Blend together in a food processor or blender until smooth and creamy:
½ pound regular tofu
2 tablespoons lemon juice
1 tablespoon dry mustard
1 teaspoon salt
¼ teaspoon freshly ground black pepper

Fold in:
½ pound regular tofu, crumbled
the onions and garlic
the broccoli florets

Bake in an oiled 9-inch quiche or pie pan for about 30 minutes, and serve hot.

Per Serving: Calories 75, Total Protein 5 g, Soy Protein 4 g,
Fat 5 g, Carbohydrates 4 g, Fiber 2 g, Calcium 156 mg, Sodium 280 mg

Mushroom Quiche

Yield: 8 servings

Preheat the oven to 350°F.

Have ready:
1 unbaked (8-inch) quiche shell

Sauté in a skillet until slightly browned:
1 tablespoon olive oil
4 cloves garlic, minced
1 medium onion, chopped
8 ounces mushrooms of choice, sliced

Blend in a food processor or blender until creamy:
1 pound regular tofu
2 tablespoons fresh lemon juice
2 tablespoons red miso, or 4 tablespoons mellow white miso
1 tablespoon Dijon mustard

Line the bottom of the quiche shell with the garlic, onion, and mushroom sauté. Pour and spread the tofu mixture on top, and bake for 40 to 45 minutes, until the top is browned and cracks start to appear around the edges.

Per Serving: Calories 197, Total Protein 6 g, Soy Protein 4 g,
Fat 11 g, Carbohydrates 15 g, Fiber 2 g, Calcium 172 mg, Sodium 195 mg

Bruchettas

Yield: 1 pound loaf (18 pieces)

Serve as a colorful side dish for soup or salad or as an appetizer.

Preheat the oven to 500°F.

Cut on the diagonal into ¾- to 1-inch slices:

1 loaf Italian or French bread baguette

Chop in a food processor or blender:

2 cloves garlic
6 tablespoons fresh basil, or a mixture of basil and chives

Add and blend until creamy:

½ pound soft or regular tofu
1 tablespoon olive oil
1 teaspoon salt

Arrange the bread slices on a baking sheet, and spread the mixture evenly over the slices. Top with:

3 to 4 thinly sliced roma tomatoes

Bake for 5 minutes until crispy and golden, and serve hot.

Per Piece: Calories 105, Total Protein 4 g, Soy Protein 1 g,
Fat 2 g, Carbohydrates 18 g, Fiber 1 g, Calcium 38 mg, Sodium 297 mg

Fried Rice with Tofu

Yield: 6 cups

This is a tasty way to serve leftover rice.

Have ready:

2 cups cooked rice
1 large onion, sliced
1 green pepper, sliced
2 ribs celery, sliced
½ pound regular tofu, diced
2 green onions, cut in ½-inch pieces

Heat in a nonstick skillet or wok:

1 tablespoon oil

Add and stir-fry for 1 minute:

the tofu cubes
1 tablespoon soy sauce

Remove the tofu and stir-fry for 3 to 4 minutes:

1 tablespoon oil
the onion slices
the green pepper slices
the celery slices

Crumble in:

the cooked rice

Add:

1 tablespoon soy sauce
the cooked tofu cubes

Stir-fry until hot. Serve sprinkled with:

the chopped green onion

Per ½ Cup: Calories 70, Total Protein 3 g, Soy Protein 2 g,
Fat 3 g, Carbohydrates 8 g, Fiber 1 g, Calcium 58 mg, Sodium 175 mg

Spanish Rice

Yield: 6 cups

Stir over medium heat until it starts to brown:
   2 tablespoons olive oil
   1½ cups uncooked long grain white rice

Pour in:
   2 cups boiling water
   1 cup picante sauce (your choice how hot)
   ½ pound firm tofu, cut in short julienne strips or crumbled
   ½ teaspoon salt

Cover and cook over high heat until it starts to boil, then turn down to low heat and cook covered for 15 to 20 minutes until the rice is tender.

Per ½ Cup: Calories 80, Total Protein 3 g, Soy Protein 1 g,
Fat 3 g, Carbohydrates 10 g, Fiber 2 g, Calcium 46 mg, Sodium 290 mg

Mexicali Rice Bake

Yield: 6 cups

Mix together and put into a 1½-quart, oiled baking dish:
   3½ cups cooked rice
   2 cups *Mock Sour Cream Dressing*, p. 52
   4 ounces dairy-free Monterey Jack cheese, grated (reserve
      enough to sprinkle over the top)
   2 (4-ounce) cans green chiles, drained and chopped
   4 to 5 drops cayenne sauce (optional)

Sprinkle the reserved cheese over the top, and bake for 15 to 20 minutes to heat through and melt the cheese on top. Baking takes longer when starting with cold rice.

Per ½ Cup: Calories 99, Total Protein 6 g, Soy Protein 5 g,
Fat 2 g, Carbohydrates 14 g, Fiber 1 g, Calcium 86 mg, Sodium 137 mg

DIPS & SPREADS

Cashew Spread ◆ 25

Cucumber-Dill Dip ◆ 28

Curried Spinach Dip ◆ 30

Curry-Chutney Dip ◆ 26

Dry Onion Soup Dip ◆ 26

Far East Dip ◆ 25

Green Dip or Spread ◆ 24

Green Goddess Dip ◆ 30

Herb Dip ◆ 29

Horseradish Dip ◆ 24

Hot Pink Dip ◆ 24

Miso Dip ◆ 28

Olive-Pecan Spread ◆ 27

Pesto Dip or Spread ◆ 29

Tartar Sauce ◆ 27

Horseradish Dip

Yield: 1¼ cups

Blend together in a food processor or blender until smooth and creamy:

½ pound soft or regular tofu
2 tablespoons lemon juice
2 tablespoons prepared horseradish
½ teaspoon salt

Per 2 Tablespoons: Calories 19, Total Protein 2 g, Soy Protein 2 g,
Fat 1 g, Carbohydrates 1 g, Fiber 0 g, Calcium 52 mg, Sodium 111 mg

Hot Pink Dip

Yield: 1½ cups

This is a zippy dip for corn chips. See photo, page 34.

Combine in a food processor or blender until creamy:

½ pound soft or regular tofu
1 (7.5-ounce) can tomatoes and jalapeños
1 tablespoon fresh lime juice
¼ teaspoon salt

Per 2 Tablespoons: Calories 13, Total Protein 1 g, Soy Protein 1 g,
Fat 0 g, Carbohydrates 1 g, Fiber 0 g, Calcium 35 mg, Sodium 88 mg

Green Dip or Spread

Yield: 1¾ cups

Use prewashed, ready-to-eat, fresh baby spinach leaves for a quick start on this dip. See photo, page 34.

Chop in a food processor or blender:

6 to 8 ounces fresh spinach

Add and blend until smooth and creamy:

½ pound regular tofu
1 tablespoon fresh lemon juice
1 package dry onion soup mix

Per 2 Tablespoons: Calories 14, Total Protein 1 g, Soy Protein 1 g,
Fat 0 g, Carbohydrates 2 g, Fiber 0 g, Calcium 31 mg, Sodium 158 mg

Far East Dip

Yield: 2 cups

Blend together in a food processor or blender until smooth and creamy:

½ pound soft or regular tofu
3 green onions, chopped (3 tablespoons)
1 tablespoon lemon juice
1 tablespoon minced candied ginger

Fold in:

¼ cup chopped walnuts
Soy sauce or salt to taste

Per 2 Tablespoons: Calories 24, Total Protein 1 g, Soy Protein 1 g,
Fat 1 g, Carbohydrates 1 g, Fiber 0 g, Calcium 36 mg, Sodium 1 mg

Cashew Spread

Yield: 1¾ cups

Chop in a food processor or by hand:

½ cup roasted salted cashews

Reserve ¼ cup to fold in at the end.

Add to the food processor or a blender, and combine until smooth and creamy:

½ pound soft or regular tofu
2 tablespoons lemon juice

Fold in the reserved chopped cashews.

Per 2 Tablespoons: Calories 44, Total Protein 2 g, Soy Protein 1 g,
Fat 4 g, Carbohydrates 2 g, Fiber 0 g, Calcium 38 mg, Sodium 36 mg

Dry Onion Soup Dip

Yield: 2¼ cups

Be sure to read the label on your soup mix to make sure it contains no animal products.

Blend in a food processor or blender until smooth and creamy:
2½ cups *Mock Sour Cream Dressing*, p. 52, omitting the salt

Stir or blend in:
1 package dry onion soup mix (scant ½ cup)

This is best if refrigerated for about 4 hours or overnight to let the flavors blend.

*Per 2 Tablespoons: Calories 25, Total Protein 2 g, Soy Protein 2 g,
Fat 1 g, Carbohydrates 2 g, Fiber 0 g, Calcium 17 mg, Sodium 130 mg*

Dry Vegetable Soup Dip: Substitute 1 package dried vegetable soup mix for the dried onion soup mix.

Dry Tomato-Onion Soup Dip: Substitute 1 package dried tomato-onion soup mix for the dried onion soup mix.

Curry-Chutney Dip

Yield: 1¾ cups

This is good with raw vegetables or spread on crackers.

Blend together in a food processor or blender until smooth and creamy:
½ pound soft or regular tofu
⅓ cup mango chutney
1 tablespoon fresh lemon juice
1 teaspoon curry powder
¼ teaspoon ground cumin
Dash of cayenne (optional)

*Per 2 Tablespoons: Calories 19, Total Protein 1 g, Soy Protein 1 g,
Fat 0 g, Carbohydrates 2 g, Fiber 0 g, Calcium 35 mg, Sodium 40 mg*

Olive-Pecan Spread

Yield: 1⅔ cups

This makes a good sandwich spread. Spread on crackers for an appetizer. See photo, page 34.

Blend in a food processor or blender until smooth and creamy.

½ pound soft or regular tofu
3 tablespoons lemon juice
¼ teaspoon salt

Fold in:

¼ cup chopped pecans
6 tablespoons sliced pimiento-stuffed olives

Per 2 Tablespoons: Calories 32, Total Protein 1 g, Soy Protein 1 g, Fat 2 g, Carbohydrates 1 g, Fiber 0 g, Calcium 40 mg, Sodium 114 mg

Tartar Sauce

Yield: 2½ cups

Chop in a food processor:

1 small onion (about ½ cup)

Add:

½ pound soft or regular tofu
¼ cup lemon juice
2 tablespoons sweetener of choice
½ teaspoon dry mustard
¾ teaspoon salt

Blend until smooth and creamy, then fold in:

¼ cup sweet pickle relish

Per 2 Tablespoons: Calories 19, Total Protein 1 g, Soy Protein 1 g, Fat 0 g, Carbohydrates 3 g, Fiber 0 g, Calcium 27 mg, Sodium 102 mg

Variation: Use dill pickle relish.

Miso Dip

Yield: ¾ cup

Try this as a spread for crackers or a dip for raw vegetables or chips.

Blend together in a blender or food processor until smooth and creamy:

¼ pound soft or regular tofu (½ cup)
1½ tablespoons sweet white miso
1 tablespoon rice vinegar
¼ teaspoon garlic powder

Variation: Use about 2 teaspoons red miso in place of the white miso.

Per 2 Tablespoons: Calories 14, Total Protein 1 g, Soy Protein 1 g,
Fat 0 g, Carbohydrates 1 g, Fiber 0 g, Calcium 21 mg, Sodium 151 mg

Cucumber-Dill Dip

Yield: 2 cups

This is a cooling dip, excellent with raw vegetables.

Blend in a food processor or blender until smooth and creamy:

½ pound soft or regular tofu
2 cucumbers, peeled, seeded, and cut up
8 green onions, chopped
3 tablespoons white wine
2 teaspoons dill weed
½ teaspoon salt
⅛ teaspoon black pepper

Per 2 Tablespoons: Calories 19, Total Protein 1 g, Soy Protein 1 g,
Fat 0 g, Carbohydrates 2 g, Fiber 1 g, Calcium 50 mg, Sodium 69 mg

Pesto Dip or Spread

Yield: 1½ cups

Serve this with chips or vegetables for dippers, or spread it on a ready-made pizza crust for Pesto Pizza, page 108 (pictured on page 105.)

Chop in a food processor:

1 to 2 cloves garlic

Add and chop:

½ cup packed fresh basil leaves
¼ cup packed fresh parsley leaves

Add and blend until smooth and creamy:

½ pound tofu
3 tablespoons pine nuts or walnuts
2 tablespoons soy Parmesan
2 tablespoons olive oil
½ teaspoon salt

Per 2 Tablespoons: Calories 52, Total Protein 2 g, Soy Protein 2 g,
Fat 4 g, Carbohydrates 1 g, Fiber 1 g, Calcium 50 mg, Sodium 115 mg

Herb Dip

Yield: about 1 cup

Blend together in a food processor or blender until smooth and creamy:

½ pound soft or regular tofu
2 tablespoons fresh parsley
1 tablespoon olive oil
½ teaspoon basil
½ teaspoon oregano
½ teaspoon salt

Per 2 Tablespoons: Calories 37, Total Protein 2 g, Soy Protein 2 g,
Fat 2 g, Carbohydrates 1 g, Fiber 0 g, Calcium 61 mg, Sodium 136 mg

Green Goddess Dip

Yield: 1½ cups

Chop in a food processor:
1 clove fresh garlic
4 green onions with tops
½ cup parsley leaves

Add and blend together until smooth and creamy:
½ pound soft or regular tofu
½ teaspoon salt
¼ teaspoon black pepper
⅛ teaspoon tarragon

Per 2 Tablespoons: Calories 16, Total Protein 1 g, Soy Protein 1 g, Fat 0 g, Carbohydrates 1 g, Fiber 0 g, Calcium 52 mg, Sodium 91 mg

Curried Spinach Dip

Yield: about 2 cups

Chop in a food processor or blender:
1 clove garlic
½ pound fresh spinach leaves

Add and blend until creamy:
½ pound regular tofu
2 tablespoons fresh lemon juice
2 tablespoons sweet white miso
1 teaspoon curry powder

Per 2 Tablespoons: Calories 20, Total Protein 2 g, Soy Protein 1 g, Fat 0 g, Carbohydrates 1 g, Fiber 1 g, Calcium 43 mg, Sodium 121 mg

Variation: Use a 10-ounce package of frozen spinach, thawed and drained, in place of the fresh spinach.

SALADS &
SALAD DRESSINGS

SALADS

Cold Curried Rice Salad ◆ 41
Cucumber-Dill Salad ◆ 42
Ensalada de Aguacate ◆ 35
Four Bean Salad ◆ 48
Garbanzo Bean Salad ◆ 40
Iowa Potato Salad ◆ 46
Lebanese Salad for Pita Pockets ◆ 38
Mock Chicken Salad ◆ 39
Pasta-Tofu Salad ◆ 45
Pineapple-Peanut Slaw ◆ 36
Pinto Bean Salad ◆ 37
Roasted Beet Salad ◆ 49
Roasted Pepper-Zucchini Salad ◆ 47
Seashell Salad ◆ 44
Sesame Spinach Salad ◆ 50
Spinach-Pine Nut Salad ◆ 37
Stuffed Avocado Salad ◆ 41
Sweet Pepper-Tofu Salad ◆ 43
Taco Salad ◆ 32
Tofu Salad for Sandwiches ◆ 43
Waldorf Salad ◆ 36

SALAD DRESSINGS

Basil-Garlic Dressing ◆ 51
Chutney Dressing ◆ 51
Cole Slaw Dressing ◆ 55
Creamy Salad Dressing ◆ 53
Cruise Ship Mustard Dressing ◆ 56
Cucumber-Dill Dressing ◆ 55
Curry Dressing ◆ 54
Fruit Salad Dressing ◆ 53
Garlic Lo-Cal Dressing ◆ 54
Mock Sour Cream Dressing ◆ 52

Taco Salad

Yield: 4 quarts

Crumble into a bowl:

1 pound firm tofu

Sprinkle with:

1 (1.75-ounce) package taco seasoning mix

Mix this all together and brown in:

2 tablespoons oil

While the tofu is browning, mix or arrange the following in a bowl:

2 tomatoes, chopped
1 small head of lettuce, torn in bite-size pieces
1 small onion, chopped
1 ripe avocado, cubed
1 cucumber, chopped
½ cup chopped black or green olives

Before serving, add:

8 ounces oven-baked corn chips
the flavored tofu

If you toss it all together, serve immediately so the chips won't get soggy. Serve with mild hot sauce for dressing.

Per 2 Cups: Calories 224, Total Protein 7 g, Soy Protein 3 g,
Fat 12 g, Carbohydrates 22 g, Fiber 3 g, Calcium 189 mg, Sodium 424 mg

Variation: Add a drained 15-ounce can of pinto or black beans to the salad, and top with *Mock Sour Cream Dressing*, page 52.

Pictured to the right from the top of the page: Scrambled Tofu Rancheros, page 16 and Whole Grain Pancakes, page 12.

Ensalada de Aguacate
(Avocado Salad)

Yield: 1½ quarts

See photo, page 67.

Mix together in a blender or jar:
  ¼ cup fresh lime juice
  2 tablespoons chopped fresh parsley or cilantro
  1 tablespoon olive oil
  1 teaspoon salt
  1 clove garlic, pressed, or ½ teaspoon garlic powder
  ¼ teaspoon black pepper

Pour this dressing over:
  ¾ pound firm tofu, cut in ½-inch or smaller cubes
  2 ripe tomatoes, chopped
  1 ripe avocado, cubed
  1 small green bell pepper, chopped
  ¼ cup chopped sweet red onion

Serve on curly or romaine lettuce, in a pita bread with lettuce, or rolled up in a flour tortilla with lettuce.

Per ½ Cup: Calories 68, Total Protein 3 g, Soy Protein 2 g,
Fat 4 g, Carbohydrates 4 g, Fiber 1 g, Calcium 65 mg, Sodium 183 mg

Pictured to the left clockwise from the top left: Hot Pink Dip, page 24, Green Dip or Spread, page 24, Olive-Pecan Spread, page 27.

Pineapple-Peanut Slaw

Yield: 6 cups

Mix together in a bowl:
   3½ cups shredded cabbage
   2 medium carrots, shredded
   1 (14-ounce) can pineapple chunks, drained,
      or about 2 cups fresh pineapple cut into chunks
   ½ cup roasted unsalted peanuts

Pour over and mix in:
   1¼ cups *Cole Slaw Dressing*, p. 55

Per ½ Cup: Calories 91, Total Protein 3 g, Soy Protein 2 g,
Fat 2 g, Carbohydrates 11 g, Fiber 2 g, Calcium 28 mg, Sodium 135 mg

Waldorf Salad

Yield 3½ cups

Here is the classic salad with a tofu dressing.

Mix together:
   2 cups chopped apples
   1 tablespoon lemon juice
   1 cup diced celery
   ½ cup chopped walnuts

Then mix in:
   1 cup *Mock Sour Cream Dressing*, p. 52

Chill and serve.

Per ½ Cup: Calories 114, Total Protein 3 g, Soy Protein 2 g,
Fat 5 g, Carbohydrates 11 g, Fiber 3 g, Calcium 28 mg, Sodium 78 mg

Spinach-Pine Nut Salad

Yield: 2 quarts

This colorful salad is pictured on the cover.

Have ready:

½ pound young spinach leaves, washed and stems removed
1 small red onion, sliced
2 ribs celery, sliced on the diagonal
½ cup pine nuts
½ pound firm tofu, cut in small cubes

To make the dressing, shake together in a small jar:

4 tablespoons olive oil
2 tablespoons wine vinegar
½ teaspoon salt
½ teaspoon dry mustard
¼ teaspoon freshly ground black pepper

Place the tofu cubes in a glass serving bowl. Pour the dressing over and toss to coat. Add the rest and toss to mix well.

Per Cup: Calories 143, Total Protein 5 g, Soy Protein 2 g,
Fat 12 g, Carbohydrates 4 g, Fiber 3 g, Calcium 96 mg, Sodium 167 mg

Pinto Bean Salad

Yield: 4 cups

Mix together in a salad bowl:

1 (15-ounce) can pinto beans, drained
1 pound firm tofu, drained and cut in small cubes
4 green onions with tops, chopped
8 small radishes, sliced
½ cup chopped celery
½ cup bottled Italian salad dressing

Mix all together and serve on red-tipped lettuce.

Per ½ Cup: Calories 188, Total Protein 8 g, Soy Protein 4 g,
Fat 9 g, Carbohydrates 18 g, Fiber 3 g, Calcium 149 mg, Sodium 128 mg

Lebanese Salad
for Pita Pockets

Yield: 6 cups

Combine in a jar:

2 tablespoons olive oil
2 tablespoons lemon juice
½ teaspoon salt
1 clove garlic, minced
A few drops hot pepper sauce

Shake and add to the jar:

1 pound firm tofu, cut in small cubes

Toss in a salad bowl:

2 cups torn lettuce or spinach leaves
1 cup cucumber, seeded and chopped
2 tomatoes, diced
½ cup chopped green onions
¼ cup currants
¼ cup chopped fresh mint
¼ cup chopped fresh parsley

Stir the tofu and dressing into the salad, and serve in warm pita breads cut in half.

Per Cup: Calories 134, Total Protein 6 g, Soy Protein 5 g,
Fat 7 g, Carbohydrates 9 g, Fiber 2 g, Calcium 184 mg, Sodium 190 mg

Mock Chicken Salad

Yield: 4 cups

Combine in a bowl:

1 pound regular or firm tofu, cut in ½-inch cubes
2 tablespoons fresh lemon juice
½ teaspoon celery salt

Mix in:

1 cup diced celery
¼ cup minced green onion
½ cup slivered, toasted almonds
½ teaspoon salt

Blend together with:

1 cup *Mock Sour Cream Dressing*, p. 52

Chill and serve.

Per ½ Cup: Calories 121, Total Protein 8 g, Soy Protein 6 g,
Fat 8 g, Carbohydrates 5 g, Fiber 2 g, Calcium 157 mg, Sodium 322 mg

Garbanzo Bean Salad

Yield: 5 cups

For the dressing, blend together:

¼ **cup olive oil**

2 tablespoons apple cider vinegar

1 teaspoon curry powder

½ **teaspoon salt, or 1½ tablespoons sweet white miso**

¼ **teaspoon freshly ground black pepper**

For the salad, mix together:

1 (20-ounce) can garbanzo beans or chick-peas, drained

½ **pound firm tofu, grated**

¾ **cup fresh or frozen green peas**

½ **cup diced celery**

2 tablespoons minced red onion

½ **ounce fresh cilantro leaves, minced (¼ cup)**

Toss and mix the salad and dressing together, then adjust the seasonings to taste. Since curry powders vary in strength and flavor, you may want to add more or less. Chill and serve on lettuce.

Per ½ Cup: Calories 171, Total Protein 7 g, Soy Protein 1 g,
Fat 7 g, Carbohydrates 19 g, Fiber 4 g, Calcium 82 mg, Sodium 119 mg

Cold Curried Rice Salad

Yield: about 2½ cups

Have ready:

1 cup *Mock Sour Cream Dressing*, p. 52
1 cup cooked leftover rice

Put the rice in a bowl, and mix in:

½ cup chopped cucumber
¼ cup chopped green pepper
¼ cup chopped green onion
3 tablespoons mango chutney
1 tablespoon lemon juice
2 teaspoons curry powder
½ teaspoon cumin

Mix in the *Sour Cream Dressing*, chill, and serve on lettuce.

Per ½ Cup: Calories 46, Total Protein 3 g, Soy Protein 3 g,
Fat 1 g, Carbohydrates 5 g, Fiber 1 g, Calcium 23 mg, Sodium 153 mg

Stuffed Avocado Salad

Yield: 4 servings

Cut in half and remove the pits from:

2 avocados

Mix together for the filling:

½ pound regular tofu, crumbled
½ teaspoon basil
¼ cup chopped pimiento
½ teaspoon salt
¼ teaspoon garlic powder
1 tablespoon red wine vinegar
¼ teaspoon freshly ground black pepper

Stuff each avocado half with ½ cup of the filling.

Per Serving: Calories 248, Total Protein 6 g, Soy Protein 4 g,
Fat 17 g, Carbohydrates 14 g, Fiber 4 g, Calcium 133 mg, Sodium 280 mg

Cucumber-Dill Salad

Yield: 6 servings

Peel and slice:

2 medium cucumbers

Sprinkle them with:

1 teaspoon salt
Ice cubes

Refrigerate for about 15 minutes, then rinse, drain, and press out the excess water.

Add:

1 small onion, chopped
1¼ cups *Mock Sour Cream Dressing*, p. 52
½ teaspoon dill weed

Mix and serve.

Per Serving: Calories 48, Total Protein 4 g, Soy Protein 3 g,
Fat 1 g, Carbohydrates 5 g, Fiber 2 g, Calcium 31 mg, Sodium 93 mg

Sweet Pepper-Tofu Salad

Yield: 4 cups

Mix together in a bowl:

1 pound regular tofu, mashed, crumbled, or coarsely grated
⅓ cup chopped red or yellow bell pepper
½ cup chopped onion
2 tablespoons chopped fresh parsley
1 teaspoon dried basil
1 teaspoon garlic powder

Pour over and mix in:

1¼ cups *Creamy Salad Dressing*, p. 53, or soy mayonnaise

Per ½ Cup: Calories 91, Total Protein 7 g, Soy Protein 6 g,
Fat 4 g, Carbohydrates 7 g, Fiber 1 g, Calcium 210 mg, Sodium 180 mg

Tofu Salad for Sandwiches

Yield: 4½ cups

This is a replacement for egg salad. See photo, page 67.

Mix together in a bowl:

1 pound regular tofu, mashed, crumbled, or coarsely grated
⅓ cup sweet pickle relish
¼ cup chopped onion, or 1 tablespoon onion powder
½ cup chopped celery
1 clove garlic, pressed, or ¼ teaspoon garlic powder
2 tablespoons nutritional yeast flakes (optional)
1 tablespoon chopped fresh parsley

Pour over and mix in:

1 cup *Creamy Salad Dressing*, p. 53, or soy mayonnaise

Per ½ Cup: Calories 80, Total Protein 5 g, Soy Protein 5 g,
Fat 3 g, Carbohydrates 7 g, Fiber 1 g, Calcium 159 mg, Sodium 190 mg

Seashell Salad

Yield: 4½ cups

Cook to al dente in boiling salted water:

1 cup small shell macaroni

Rinse with cold water and drain.

Mix the shells in a bowl with:

1 cup cocktail sauce
¾ pound regular or firm tofu, cut in small cubes
½ cup chopped green pepper
½ cup chopped green onion
¼ cup chopped celery
¼ cup soy mayonnaise or *Creamy Salad Dressing,* **p. 53**

Serve on a bed of lettuce.

Per ½ Cup: Calories 121, Total Protein 5 g, Soy Protein 3 g,
Fat 2 g, Carbohydrates 18 g, Fiber 1 g, Calcium 93 mg, Sodium 391 mg

Pasta-Tofu Salad

Yield: 7 cups

Cook in boiling salted water to al dente:

8 ounces spiral noodles

Rinse with cold water and drain.

Mix together in a salad bowl:

½ pound firm tofu, coarsely grated
½ cup chopped celery
4 green onions with tops, chopped

Toss all together with the noodles.

Mix in:

2 cups *Cruise Ship Mustard Dressing*, p. 56

Garnish with:

**1 (8-ounce) can asparagus tips, drained, or 1 (8-ounce) can
artichoke hearts, drained**

*Per Cup: Calories 135, Total Protein 9 g, Soy Protein 7 g,
Fat 5 g, Carbohydrates 12 g, Fiber 2 g, Calcium 100 mg, Sodium 486 mg*

Iowa Potato Salad

Yield: 5½ cups

Scrub well and cut up:
  4 medium potatoes (1½ pounds)

Boil in salted water until tender. Drain and slip the skins off, and break or cut into pieces. (If the potatoes are well scrubbed, the skins can be left on.)

While the potatoes are still hot, toss with a mixture of
  2 tablespoons olive oil
  2 tablespoons apple cider vinegar
  ½ teaspoon salt
  ⅛ teaspoon black pepper

Let cool. Add to the cooled potatoes:
  ⅓ cup minced onion
  1½ cups diced celery
  ¼ cup minced parsley
  Celery salt to taste

To make the dressing, combine in a blender or food processor:
  ½ (12.3-ounce) package firm silken tofu
  3 tablespoons apple cider vinegar
  ¼ teaspoon garlic powder
  ½ teaspoon onion powder
  ½ teaspoon sweetener of choice

Mix the dressing into the salad, chill, and serve.

Per ½ Cup: Calories 117, Total Protein 1 g, Soy Protein 0 g,
Fat 5 g, Carbohydrates 15 g, Fiber 2 g, Calcium 12 mg, Sodium 220 mg

Variation: You can substitute ¾ cup soy mayonnaise for the homemade dressing.

Roasted Pepper-Zucchini Salad

Yield: about 2 quarts

Add other vegetables to the roasting pan, if you like. This salad is pictured on page 69.

Toss the vegetables with the olive oil below, and roast at 350°F for 15 to 20 minutes until tender:

1 pound bell peppers in assorted colors, cut in bite size pieces
¾ pound zucchini, cut in ¼-inch-thick slices
1 onion, cut in ¾-inch pieces
6 cloves garlic, unpeeled
1 teaspoon olive oil

In the last 10 minutes add to the oven:

½ cup almonds

Peel and chop the garlic after it has been roasted, chop the almonds, and toss with the roasted vegetables in a salad bowl.

While the vegetables are roasting, cook in boiling salted water to al dente, then drain:

½ pound bow tie or fusilli noodles

Add the pasta to the vegetables in the salad bowl, and toss with:

½ pound extra-firm tofu, grated
½ ounce minced fresh basil
½ cup prepared, low-fat Italian salad dressing

Per Cup: Calories 156, Total Protein 5 g, Soy Protein 2 g, Fat 8 g, Carbohydrates 15 g, Fiber 3 g, Calcium 99 mg, Sodium 125 mg

Four Bean Salad

Yield: 2 quarts

Blend together in food processor, blender, or jar:
¼ cup olive oil
¼ cup cider vinegar
1 teaspoon oregano
1 teaspoon basil
1 teaspoon salt
½ teaspoon dry mustard
½ teaspoon freshly ground black pepper

Mix together in a bowl:
½ pound firm tofu, cut in small cubes
1 small onion, chopped
1 rib celery, chopped
1 (10-ounce) package frozen green beans, cooked

Pour the dressing over the green beans while they are hot, and stir in:
1 (15-ounce) can kidney beans, drained and rinsed
1 (15-ounce) can garbanzo beans, drained and rinsed

Mix together, and marinate overnight.

Per ½ Cup: Calories 115, Total Protein 5 g, Soy Protein 1 g,
Fat 5 g, Carbohydrates 14 g, Fiber 3 g, Calcium 67 mg, Sodium 140 mg

Variation: Replace the cooked green beans with cooked edamame (green soybeans).

Roasted Beet Salad

Yield: about 4 cups

Make this bright pink salad a day ahead so the flavors will blend together.

Preheat the oven to 400°F.

Wash, peel, and slice into thin slices:

1 pound beets

Toss the beet slices with:

1 tablespoon olive oil

Spread them out on a baking sheet, and roast for 10 to 15 minutes until tender.

While the beets are cooking, mix together:

½ cup orange juice
¼ cup apple cider vinegar
1 tablespoon olive oil
1 tablespoon sweetener of choice
1 tablespoon sweet white miso
1 teaspoon organic orange zest

Pour this mixture over the hot roasted beets in a glass or stainless bowl, then gently mix in:

½ pound firm tofu, cut into ¼-inch cubes
½ medium onion, thinly sliced

Marinate overnight, gently stirring occasionally, and serve cold on a bed of lettuce.

Per ½ Cup: Calories 95, Total Protein 3 g, Soy Protein 3 g,
Fat 5 g, Carbohydrates 10 g, Fiber 2 g, Calcium 68 mg, Sodium 139 mg

Sesame Spinach Salad

Yield: 2 quarts

Have ready:

½ pound spinach leaves, washed
½ pound red tip or leaf lettuce
¼ cup chopped red onion
½ pound firm tofu, cut in ½-inch cubes

To make the dressing, mix together in a jar:

2 tablespoons olive oil
2 tablespoons white wine vinegar
1 tablespoon soy sauce
¼ teaspoon powdered ginger
¼ teaspoon garlic powder
¼ teaspoon black pepper

Heat in a skillet:

1 tablespoon sesame oil

Add and brown while stirring:

2 tablespoons sesame seeds

Add and stir to coat with seeds:

the tofu cubes

Pour the dressing into the pan, mix, and turn off the heat. Combine the tofu and torn-up greens in a 3-quart bowl, tossing gently. Serve immediately.

Garnish with:

2 tablespoons vegan bacon bits (optional), and/or add salt to taste.

Per Cup: Calories 95, Total Protein 3 g, Soy Protein 2 g,
Fat 7 g, Carbohydrates 3 g, Fiber 2 g, Calcium 131 mg, Sodium 153 mg

SALAD DRESSINGS

Basil-Garlic Dressing

Yield: 1½ cups

Chop in a food processor:
   2 cloves garlic

Add and chop:
   ¾ cup chopped, loosely packed fresh basil

Add and blend until smooth and creamy:
   1 (12.3-ounce) package soft silken tofu
   2 tablespoons olive oil
   2 tablespoons red wine vinegar
   ½ teaspoon salt

   *Per 2 Tablespoons: Calories 36, Total Protein 1 g, Soy Protein 1 g,
   Fat 3 g, Carbohydrates 1 g, Fiber 0 g, Calcium 11 mg, Sodium 91 mg*

Chutney Dressing

Yield: 1¾ cups

Blend together in a food processor or blender until smooth and creamy:
   ½ pound soft tofu
   3 tablespoons chutney
   1 tablespoon lemon juice
   ½ teaspoon salt
   ¼ cup water

   *Per 2 Tablespoons: Calories 16, Total Protein 1 g, Soy Protein 1 g,
   Fat 0 g, Carbohydrates 2 g, Fiber 0 g, Calcium 34 mg, Sodium 100 mg*

Mock Sour Cream Dressing

This low-calorie, no-cholesterol dressing can be used in a variety of recipes that call for sour cream. Here are two different versions.

Yield: 1½ cups

Combine in a blender or food processor until smooth and creamy:

1 (12.3-ounce) package firm silken tofu

2 tablespoons lemon juice

¼ teaspoon salt

Per 2 Tablespoons: Calories 18, Total Protein 2 g, Soy Protein 2 g,
Fat 1 g, Carbohydrates 1 g, Fiber 0 g, Calcium 11 mg, Sodium 54 mg

Yield: 1¾ cups

Combine in a blender or food processor until smooth and creamy:

½ pound regular tofu

½ cup soy yogurt

2 tablespoons lemon juice

½ teaspoon salt

Per 2 Tablespoons: Calories 16, Total Protein 1 g, Soy Protein 1 g,
Fat 0 g, Carbohydrates 1 g, Fiber 0 g, Calcium 34 mg, Sodium 78 mg

Creamy Salad Dressing

Yield: 1 cup

Here is a low-calorie, no-cholesterol substitute for mayonnaise.

Combine in a food processor or blender until smooth and creamy:
½ pound soft tofu
1 teaspoon Dijon mustard (optional)
½ teaspoon salt
3 tablespoons apple cider vinegar
¼ teaspoon black pepper
1 tablespoon sweetener of choice

Per 2 Tablespoons: Calories 29, Total Protein 2 g, Soy Protein 2 g,
Fat 1 g, Carbohydrates 2 g, Fiber 0 g, Calcium 58 mg, Sodium 135 mg

Fruit Salad Dressing

Yield: 1⅓ cups

This was inspired by a fruit salad dressing my mother used to make.

Combine in a blender or food processor until smooth and creamy:
½ (12.3-ounce) package soft silken tofu
¼ cup sweetener of choice
⅓ cup apple cider vinegar
1½ tablespoons minced onion
2 teaspoons celery seed
¼ teaspoon dry mustard
1 teaspoon salt
1 teaspoon paprika

Per 2 Tablespoons: Calories 27, Total Protein 1 g, Soy Protein 1 g,
Fat 0 g, Carbohydrates 5 g, Fiber 0 g, Calcium 5 mg, Sodium 195 mg

Curry Dressing

Yield: ¾ cup

This makes a good dressing for fruit salad.

Combine in a food processor or blender until smooth and creamy:

½ (12.3-ounce) package soft silken tofu
3 tablespoons fresh lemon juice
1 tablespoon sweetener of choice
½ teaspoon curry powder
¼ teaspoon ginger
¼ teaspoon salt

Per 2 Tablespoons: Calories 25, Total Protein 1 g, Soy Protein 1 g,
Fat 1 g, Carbohydrates 3 g, Fiber 0 g, Calcium 9 mg, Sodium 91 mg

Garlic Lo-Cal Dressing

Yield: 1¼ cups

See photo, page 67.

Chop in a food processor:

2 small cloves garlic

Add and blend until smooth and creamy:

½ (12.3-ounce) package lite, soft silken tofu
¼ cup white vinegar
½ teaspoon salt
¼ teaspoon dry mustard (optional)
¼ teaspoon black pepper

Per 2 Tablespoons: Calories 9, Total Protein 1 g, Soy Protein 1 g,
Fat 0 g, Carbohydrates 1 g, Fiber 0 g, Calcium 3 mg, Sodium 123 mg

Pink Lo-Cal Dressing: Blend in ¼ cup ketchup with the rest of the ingredients.

Cole Slaw Dressing

Yield: about 1¼ cups

This creamy dressing will cover 4 cups shredded vegetables.

Chop in a blender or food processor:
- **1 clove garlic**
- **1 tablespoon chopped onion**

Add to the blender and blend until all is smooth and creamy:
- **½ (12.3-ounce) package soft silken tofu**
- **3 tablespoons cider vinegar**
- **2 tablespoons sweetener of choice**
- **1 tablespoon mellow barley miso, or ½ teaspoon salt**
- **⅛ teaspoon black pepper**

Per 2 Tablespoons: Calories 25, Total Protein 1 g, Soy Protein 1 g, Fat 1 g, Carbohydrates 3 g, Fiber 0 g, Calcium 7 mg, Sodium 88 mg

Cucumber-Dill Dressing

Yield: 2½ cups

Combine in a food processor or blender until smooth and creamy:
- **½ pound soft tofu**
- **1 medium cucumber, peeled and cut in 8 pieces**
- **2 tablespoons white rice vinegar**
- **1 teaspoon dill weed**
- **½ teaspoon salt**
- **¼ teaspoon black pepper**

Per 2 Tablespoons: Calories 11, Total Protein 1 g, Soy Protein 1 g, Fat 0 g, Carbohydrates 1 g, Fiber 0 g, Calcium 25 mg, Sodium 54 mg

Cruise Ship Mustard Dressing

Yield: ¾ cup

Combine in a food processor or blender:

½ (12.3-ounce) package soft silken tofu
2 tablespoons Dijon mustard
2 tablespoons lemon juice
1 tablespoon soy Parmesan

Per 2 Tablespoons: Calories 44, Total Protein 3 g, Soy Protein 3 g,
Fat 3 g, Carbohydrates 2 g, Fiber 0 g, Calcium 13 mg, Sodium 166 mg

SOUPS

Chunky Gazpacho ✦ 64

Cool Cucumber-Avocado Soup ✦ 65

Corn Chowder ✦ 60

Gumbo Soup ✦ 58

Lentil Soup ✦ 71

Miso Vegetable Soup ✦ 62

Potato Tofu Soup ✦ 72

Pumpkin Soup ✦ 71

Quick Vegetable Tofu Soup ✦ 59

Ramen Noodle Soup ✦ 63

Southwestern Chili ✦ 61

Spinach Soup ✦ 66

Gumbo Soup

Yield: 6 cups

Have ready:

½ pound frozen tofu, thawed, gently squeezed dry, and chopped

Bubble together in a heavy-bottom soup pan until the color of peanut butter:

2 tablespoons oil
2 tablespoons flour

Stir in:

2 cups water
3 teaspoons vegetable bouillon powder

Bring to a boil and add:

1 pound frozen vegetable gumbo mixture
the tofu
1 (15-ounce) can peeled tomatoes, chopped, with juice
1 bay leaf

Stir, cover, and bring to a boil. Let simmer for 18 to 20 minutes until the vegetables are tender. Serve with hot cooked rice.

Per Cup: Calories 108, Total Protein 4 g, Soy Protein 3 g,
Fat 6 g, Carbohydrates 9 g, Fiber 3 g, Calcium 102 mg, Sodium 121 mg

Quick Vegetable Tofu Soup

Yield: 4 cups

Bring to a boil in a small saucepan:

4½ cups water

Add:

¼ pound regular tofu, cut in small cubes

When the water boils again, stir in with a wire whisk:

1 (1.4-ounce) package dry vegetable soup mix

Reduce the heat to low, and simmer for 20 minutes.

Per Cup: Calories 50, Total Protein 2 g, Soy Protein 2 g,
Fat 1 g, Carbohydrates 8 g, Fiber 0 g, Calcium 57 mg, Sodium 755 mg

Corn Chowder

Yield: 2 quarts

See photo, page 68.

Have ready:

  2 onions, chopped
  1 red or green bell pepper, chopped
  2 ribs celery, chopped
  2 small potatoes, cut in ½-inch cubes
  2 cloves garlic, pressed

Heat in a saucepan:

  1 tablespoon oil

Add all the chopped vegetables, stir, and cook until the onions are transparent.

Then add:

  4 cups water
  1 small bay leaf
  ¼ teaspoon thyme

When it comes to a boil and the vegetables are almost tender, add:

  4 teaspoons vegetable bouillon powder
  2½ cups frozen corn
  ½ pound regular or firm tofu, cut in ¼-inch cubes
  ¼ teaspoon freshly ground black pepper

Serve when the corn is tender. Garnish with red and green bell pepper rings and fresh cilantro.

Per Cup: Calories 150, Total Protein 6 g, Soy Protein 2 g,
Fat 4 g, Carbohydrates 21 g, Fiber 5 g, Calcium 105 mg, Sodium 92 mg

Southwestern Chili

Yield: 7 cups

If you have leftover chili, try using it as a topping for baked potatoes.

Have ready:

1 pound frozen tofu, thawed, gently squeezed dry, and torn into bite-size pieces

Sauté in a 2½- to 3-quart soup pot:

1 tablespoon oil
1 medium green pepper, diced
1 medium onion, diced
2 cloves garlic, minced

When they are almost tender, add:

the tofu pieces
1½ tablespoons chili powder
1 teaspoon cumin
1 teaspoon salt
Chipotle powder to taste

Sauté all together until the vegetables are tender, then add:

1 (30-ounce) can pinto or kidney beans, rinsed and drained
3 cups water
½ cup chopped fresh cilantro

Heat thoroughly and serve.

Per Cup: Calories 171, Total Protein 10 g, Soy Protein 5 g,
Fat 5 g, Carbohydrates 21 g, Fiber 5 g, Calcium 185 mg, Sodium 817 mg

Miso Vegetable Soup

Yield: 6 cups

Sauté together for a couple of minutes:
½ tablespoon olive oil
½ cup sliced onion
½ cup sliced carrot
½ cup sliced celery

Add:
6 cups boiling water
¼ pound chopped fresh or frozen spinach or shredded napa cabbage
¼ pound regular or firm tofu, cut in small cubes

Bring back to a boil, and cook until the vegetables are tender. Dissolve together:
1 cup hot water
¼ cup sweet white or chick-pea miso

Turn off the heat, pour the miso mixture into the pot, and stir. Serve hot.

Per Cup: Calories 67, Total Protein 4 g, Soy Protein 3 g,
Fat 2 g, Carbohydrates 6 g, Fiber 1 g, Calcium 66 mg, Sodium 608 mg

Ramen Noodle Soup

Yield: 2½ cups per package

There are several brands of packaged ramen noodle soups. They contain ready-to-cook noodles and a prepared flavoring mixture. Look for brands that contain no MSG or hydrolyzed vegetable protein. To keep the fat content down, look for noodles that are not fried. With your added tofu and vegetables, this becomes a quick and easy lunch, snack, or light supper. Start by preparing any vegetables you'd like to have in the soup, or whatever you have on hand: carrots, onion, broccoli, cabbage, greens, parsley, and so on. Leftovers are okay; they won't have to be cooked. Try using something from the supermarket salad bar already chopped. If you are chopping your own, slice everything very thin so it will cook quickly. If you have leftover cooked vegetables, save them to add last.

For each serving have ready:

½ cup thinly sliced raw vegetables
½ ounce fresh or frozen tofu, cut into ½ inch cubes or strips

Bring the water called for on the package to a boil. Add the thinly sliced vegetables, noodles, and tofu. When the noodles are done, turn off the heat and add the flavoring and any leftover vegetables you want to add. Serve garnished with chopped green onion.

*Per Cup: Calories 158, Total Protein 3 g, Soy Protein 1 g,
Fat 1 g, Carbohydrates 12 g, Fiber 1 g, Calcium 49 mg, Sodium 699 mg*

Chunky Gazpacho

Yield: 6 cups

Mix together in a bowl:

    3 cups peeled and chopped fresh tomatoes
    ½ pound regular tofu, cut in small cubes
    2 cups tomato juice
    1 medium cucumber, seeded and chopped (about 1¼ cups)
    ⅓ cup minced green pepper
    ¼ cup minced green onion
    1½ tablespoons minced fresh parsley
    1 tablespoon olive oil
    1 tablespoon red wine vinegar
    1 teaspoon salt
    ¼ teaspoon garlic powder
    ¼ teaspoon basil
    ¼ teaspoon oregano
    ⅛ teaspoon black pepper

Chill and serve.

Per Cup: Calories 93, Total Protein 4 g, Soy Protein 3 g,
Fat 4 g, Carbohydrates 10 g, Fiber 3 g, Calcium 115 mg, Sodium 259 mg

Variation: Use canned tomatoes when fresh tomatoes are out of season.

Cool Cucumber-Avocado Soup

Yield: 3 cups

This is a refreshing, cool soup for a hot summer's day.

Have all the ingredients cold before starting.

Process in a blender until smooth and creamy:
   1 small clove garlic
   3 tablespoons chopped fresh cilantro or basil
   1 pound cucumber, peeled, seeded, and cut into chunks
   ½ ripe Haas avocado
   ½ (12.3-ounce) package silken tofu
   1 tablespoon fresh lime juice
   ¼ ounce fresh jalapeño, or to taste
   2 tablespoons sweet white miso

If the soup is too thick, add several ice cubes to the blender and process until crushed. Garnish with red bell pepper strips, and serve with corn chips.

Per Cup Serving: Calories 144, Total Protein 7 g, Soy Protein 4 g, Fat 5 g, Carbohydrates 13 g, Fiber 4 g, Calcium 45 mg, Sodium 606 mg

Spinach Soup

Yield: 4 cups

Have ready:

1 (10-ounce) package frozen spinach, thawed and drained
3 cups vegetable bouillon
½ cup instant mashed potato flakes

Sauté together:

1 tablespoon olive oil
2 tablespoons chopped onion

Remove from the heat and crumble in:

½ pound regular tofu

Pour the vegetable bouillon over the spinach in a large saucepan and heat.

Stir together:

½ cup soymilk
½ cup of the vegetable broth

Pour this over the instant mashed potato flakes, and fluff with a fork. Stir this together with the rest of the bouillon and spinach. Process half at a time in a food processor along with:

½ cup soymilk, if necessary, to thin

Return to the saucepan. Serve hot, but do not boil.

Per Cup: Calories 206, Total Protein 8 g, Soy Protein 5 g,
Fat 6 g, Carbohydrates 27 g, Fiber 7 g, Calcium 229 mg, Sodium 323 mg

Pictured to the right: Ensalada de Aguacate (Avocado Salad), page 35, Garlic Lo-Cal Dressing, page 54, Tofu Salad for Sandwiches, page 43.

Pictured on page 68: Corn Chowder, page 60.

Pumpkin Soup

Yield: 7 cups

Sauté in a 2½-quart soup pot:

2 tablespoons oil
2 cups cubed potatoes
1 medium onion, chopped
3 cloves garlic, minced

When the potatoes are almost soft, add:

½ pound regular tofu, cut in cubes

Sprinkle well with:

1½ teaspoons salt
½ teaspoon black pepper

When the potatoes are soft, stir in:

1 (16-ounce) can pumpkin
3 cups water

Heat thoroughly and serve.

Per Cup: Calories 127, Total Protein 3 g, Soy Protein 3 g,
Fat 6 g, Carbohydrates 16 g, Fiber 3 g, Calcium 94 mg, Sodium 465 mg

Lentil Soup

Yield: 3 cups

Add tofu to already prepared soups for added protein.

Heat together:

1 (19-ounce) can lentil soup
⅓ pound regular or firm tofu, cut in small cubes

Per Cup: Calories 180, Total Protein 11 g, Soy Protein 3 g,
Fat 7 g, Carbohydrates 17 g, Fiber 3 g, Calcium 112 mg, Sodium 748 mg

Pictured on page 69: top of the page Roasted Pepper-Zucchini Salad page 47, bottom Quick Garden Wraps, page 113.

Pictured to the left: Amandine Tofu, page 82.

Potato Tofu Soup

Yield: 8 cups

Use white, red, or Yukon gold potatoes for this creamy soup.

Cook together in a soup pot until tender (about 20 minutes):

4 cups boiling water

2 teaspoons salt

2 pounds potatoes, cut in quarters (about 4 cups)

While the potatoes are cooking, sauté together until caramelized:

1 tablespoon olive oil

1 large onion, chopped

2 cloves garlic, minced

Blend in a food processor or blender until creamy:

1 (12.3-ounce) package soft silken tofu

When the potatoes are done, remove them from the pot with a slotted spoon and pull the skins off. Add them to the tofu in the processor or blender, along with the caramelized onions. Blend them together until creamy, adding some of the cooking water if necessary, then pour everything back into the pot with the potato cooking water. Stir in:

¼ teaspoon freshly ground black pepper, or to taste

Adjust the seasoning to taste, and heat to simmering, but do not boil. Serve hot with 1 teaspoon nonhydrogenated margarine and 2 tablespoons chopped parsley for each serving.

Per Cup: Calories 143, Total Protein 4 g, Soy Protein 2 g,
Fat 2 g, Carbohydrates 25 g, Fiber 3 g, Calcium 26 mg, Sodium 542 mg

Amandine Tofu ◆ 82
Angel Hair Primavera ◆ 97
Baked Potatoes with Chili Topping ◆ 87

MAIN DISHES

Baked Stuffed Potatoes ◆ 116
Barbecue Tofu ◆ 78
Breading Mixes ◆ 77
Broccoli-Mushroom Stir-Fry ◆ 86
Burritos Fritos ◆ 89
Cabbage-Tofu Stir-Fry ◆ 84
Chewy Chili ◆ 97
Chile Quiles ◆ 87
Chinese Fried Rice with Tofu ◆ 102
Curried Basmati Rice ◆ 110
Curry ◆ 101
Deviled Tofu ◆ 107
Enchilada Casserole ◆ 88
Fajitas ◆ 100
Golden Rice Pilaf ◆ 111
Green Rice ◆ 81
Hawaiian Stir-Fry ◆ 95
Lasagne ◆ 90
Lasagne Florentine ◆ 91
Lasagne with Dairy-Free Cheese ◆ 92
Macaroni & Tofu ◆ 80
Noodles Romanoff ◆ 96
Orange Tofu ◆ 79
Oriental Stir-Fry ◆ 98
Oven-Fried Tofu ◆ 76
Pesto Pizza ◆ 108
Pizza with Tofu ◆ 108
Quick & Easy Fried Tofu ◆ 74
Quick Garden Wraps ◆ 113
Sloppy Joes ◆ 112
Southwestern Pizza ◆ 109
Spring Rolls ◆ 93
Stuffed Shells ◆ 83
Stroganoff ◆ 85
Tamale Pie ◆ 94
Tofu Alfredo ◆ 89
Tofu Burgers ◆ 75
Tofu Spanakopita ◆ 114
Tofu Tacos ◆ 99

Quick & Easy Fried Tofu

Yield: 8 slices

Perhaps the quickest and easiest way to serve tofu hot for a meal or snack is to fry it. The flavor it takes on depends on what flavoring is added to it either before or while it is cooking. The tofu can be cut in cubes or crumbled instead of sliced.

Cut into 8 slices:

1 pound regular or firm tofu

Pour in a shallow dish:

2 teaspoons soy sauce

Dip each slice in the soy sauce, and then brown on each side in a nonstick skillet:

1 tablespoon oil

While it is cooking, sprinkle with any of the following to taste:

Garlic powder
Oregano
Onion powder
Poultry seasoning
Basil
Curry powder
Nutritional yeast flakes

Serve with noodles, rice, millet, buckwheat groats, potatoes, or in sandwiches.

Variation: Instead of dipping the slices in soy sauce, try spreading each slice with a thin layer of Vegemite, Marmite, or miso before frying.

Per Slice: Calories 59, Total Protein 4 g, Soy Protein 4 g, Fat 4 g, Carbohydrates 1 g, Fiber 0 g, Calcium 115 mg, Sodium 88 mg

Breaded & Fried Tofu: After dipping the tofu slices in soy sauce, dredged in any of the breadings listed for *Oven-Fried Tofu*, pages 76-77, and then pan fry.

Tofu Burgers

Yield: 8 burgers

Mix together in a bowl:

1 pound regular or firm tofu, mashed or crumbled
½ cup oatmeal
1 teaspoon salt
½ cup wheat germ
1 teaspoon poultry seasoning
2 tablespoons onion powder, or ½ teaspoon basil and
   ½ teaspoon oregano
1½ tablespoons chopped fresh parsley
½ teaspoon garlic powder

Shape into 8 burgers and brown in:

2 tablespoons oil

Serve on buns with all the fixings.

Per Burger: Calories 121, Total Protein 7 g, Soy Protein 4 g,
Fat 7 g, Carbohydrates 8 g, Fiber 2 g, Calcium 119 mg, Sodium 271 mg

Tofu Spaghetti Balls: Shape the mix into 20 balls, and carefully brown in oil.

Tofu Loaf: Press the mix into an oiled loaf pan, top with ¼ cup ketchup, and bake at 350°F for about 30 minutes. Let it cool for about 10 minutes before slicing. This makes good sandwiches cold or refried.

Oven-Fried Tofu

Yield: 8 slices

Keep one or more of these breadings for baked tofu on hand in a covered container for quick preparation.

Preheat the oven to 375°F.

Cut into 8 slices:

1 pound firm tofu

Mix together in a bowl for breading:

⅓ cup flour or bread crumbs
2 tablespoons nutritional yeast flakes
1 tablespoon onion powder
¼ teaspoon poultry seasoning
⅛ teaspoon garlic powder

Pour into a flat bowl:

2 teaspoons soy sauce

Spread a cookie sheet with:

1 tablespoon oil

Dip each slice of tofu into the soy sauce on both sides, and then dredge in breading mixture using the one-hand-wet and one-hand-dry method. Arrange breaded slices on the oiled cookie sheet. Bake for 15 minutes on one side, then about 10 minutes on the other, or until both sides are browned. Add more oil to the pan if needed when you flip the pieces. Serve like "cutlets" or in sandwiches.

Per Slice: Calories 82, Total Protein 5 g, Soy Protein 4 g,
Fat 4 g, Carbohydrates 5 g, Fiber 0 g, Calcium 127 mg, Sodium 90 mg

Onion-Mushroom Breading Mix

Mix together:

¼ cup flour or bread crumbs

1 package dry onion-mushroom soup mix

Tomato-Onion Breading Mix

Mix together:

2 tablespoons bread crumbs

1 package dry tomato-onion soup mix

Chili-Style Breading Mix

Mix together:

⅓ cup flour or breadcrumbs

1 tablespoon onion powder

1 teaspoon chile powder

1 teaspoon parsley flakes

¼ teaspoon garlic powder

Italian-Style Breading Mix

Mix together:

⅓ cup flour

1 tablespoon onion powder

½ teaspoon basil

½ teaspoon garlic powder

Barbecue Tofu

Yield: 12 ribs or 8 slices

These ribs can be served as a main dish or cut smaller for an appetizer.

Preheat the oven or toaster oven to 400°F.

Have ready:

1 pound frozen tofu, thawed, gently squeezed dry, and cut into rib-like strips, or 1 pound fresh firm tofu cut in 8 slices
¾ cup of your favorite barbecue sauce

Oil a 9- x 13-inch pan (smaller for a toaster oven) with:

1 tablespoon oil

Lay the pieces of tofu in the pan, leaving space between each one. Bake for 10 to 15 minutes or until browned on one side, then turn over and bake about 5 to 10 minutes to brown the other side. Pour and spread the barbecue sauce over all the pieces, and bake for 5 to 10 more minutes. Cooking can also be done on an outdoor grill. Serve on Kaiser rolls or with rice or potatoes. *Barbecue Tofu* can be frozen and reheated later.

Per Rib: Calories 59, Total Protein 3 g, Soy Protein 3 g,
Fat 2 g, Carbohydrates 6 g, Fiber 0 g, Calcium 79 mg, Sodium 233 mg

Orange Tofu

Yield: 8 slices

Cut into 8 slices:

1 pound firm tofu

Mix together:

⅓ cup unbleached flour
1 teaspoon paprika
1 teaspoon thyme
1 teaspoon salt
¼ teaspoon black pepper

Dredge the tofu slices in the flour mixture, then lightly brown on each side in:

1 tablespoon oil

While the tofu is cooking, mix together:

1 cup juice from 1 to 2 organic navel oranges
2 teaspoons grated rind from the organic oranges

Remove the tofu slices to a serving platter, and pour the juice mixture over the top. Fresh orange slices make a nice garnish.

Per Slice: Calories 89, Total Protein 5 g, Soy Protein 4 g,
Fat 4 g, Carbohydrates 8 g, Fiber 0 g, Calcium 127 mg, Sodium 271 mg

Macaroni & Tofu
with Dairy-Free Cheese

Yield: 4 cups

Bring to a boil:
6 cups boiling salted water

Add and boil until al dente:
6 ounces macaroni (1½ cups)

Rinse and drain.

While the macaroni is cooking, gently bubble together over low heat in a 2-quart saucepan:
2 tablespoons oil
2 tablespoons unbleached white flour
2 tablespoons nutritional yeast flakes
½ teaspoon garlic powder

Whip in, leaving no lumps:
1 cup soymilk

Stir in:
4 ounces dairy-free cheddar-style cheese, shredded (1 cup)

Stir until melted, heating if necessary. Stir in:
½ pound regular tofu, crumbled
the drained macaroni
1 teaspoon salt

Serve hot.

Per ½ Cup: Calories 129, Total Protein 8 g, Soy Protein 6 g,
Fat 7 g, Carbohydrates 9 g, Fiber 1 g, Calcium 171 mg, Sodium 392 mg

Green Rice

Yield: 4 cups

Preheat the oven to 350°F.

Have ready:

2 cups cooked white or brown rice
1 (10-ounce) package frozen spinach, thawed and drained

Sauté together:

1 tablespoon olive oil
1 medium onion, chopped
2 cloves garlic, chopped

Blend together with a wire whisk:

1 (12.3-ounce) package firm silken tofu
2 tablespoons fresh lemon juice
1 tablespoon mellow barley or brown rice miso (optional)
½ teaspoon salt, or to taste
¼ teaspoon nutmeg
⅛ teaspoon freshly ground black pepper

Mix everything together along with:

½ cup sliced almonds (optional)

Pour into a 1½-quart baking dish, and bake for about 30 minutes. Serve hot.

Per ½ Cup: Calories 109, Total Protein 5 g, Soy Protein 3 g, Fat 2 g, Carbohydrates 16 g, Fiber 3 g, Calcium 75 mg, Sodium 180 mg

Amandine Tofu

Yield: 8 slices

See photo, page 70.

Cut into 8 slices:

½ pound firm tofu

Mix together:

⅓ cup unbleached flour
1 teaspoon paprika
1 teaspoon salt
¼ teaspoon freshly ground black pepper

Dredge the tofu slices in the flour mixture, then brown in a non-stick skillet on both sides in:

1 tablespoon oil

Remove to a warm serving plate, and sprinkle with:

Juice of ½ fresh lemon

Cover with:

½ cup toasted slivered almonds

Per Slice: Calories 89, Total Protein 4 g, Soy Protein 2 g,
Fat 6 g, Carbohydrates 6 g, Fiber 1 g, Calcium 83 mg, Sodium 269 mg

Stuffed Shells

See photo on the front cover.

Have ready:
1 (26-ounce) jar of your favorite low-sodium pasta sauce

Boil in salted water to al dente:
6 ounces jumbo pasta shells (about 20 shells)

Mix together:
6 tablespoons minced fresh basil
¼ cup chopped fresh parsley
1 to 2 cloves fresh garlic, minced
1½ pounds regular tofu, mashed, or 1 pound regular tofu,
mashed and ½ pound dairy-free mozzarella, grated
2 tablespoons onion powder
1½ teaspoons salt

Spread ⅔ of the pasta sauce on the bottom of a shallow 2½- to -3-quart baking dish. Spoon the tofu mixture into the cooked shells, about ⅓ cup per shell, and arrange in the pan. Add ½ cup water to the remaining sauce, then pour stripes of sauce over the tops of the shells. Top with optional soy Parmesan, and bake at 350°F until the pasta sauce is bubbly, about 25 minutes.

Per Serving: Calories 125, Total Protein 9 g, Soy Protein 6 g,
Fat 4 g, Carbohydrates 13 g, Fiber 4 g, Calcium 197 mg, Sodium 436 mg

Cabbage-Tofu Stir-Fry

Yield: 6 cups

Have ready:

2 tablespoons sesame seeds
1 teaspoon chopped fresh ginger
6 cups shredded savoy or Chinese cabbage
1 pound firm tofu, cut into ¾-inch cubes

to make the sauce, mix together and set aside:

2 tablespoons white wine vinegar
2 tablespoons soy sauce
1 tablespoon sesame oil
2 teaspoons cornstarch
1 teaspoon sweetener of choice

Heat in a wok:

1 tablespoon oil

Add the sesame seeds and ginger, and stir-fry for 1 minute. Add the cabbage and stir-fry for 2 to 3 minutes. Add the tofu and stir-fry 1 more minute. Pour in the sauce and cook 1 minute more, stirring to coat. Serve with rice or noodles.

Per Cup: Calories 141, Total Protein 7 g, Soy Protein 6 g,
Fat 8 g, Carbohydrates 8 g, Fiber 2 g, Calcium 217 mg, Sodium 353 mg

Stroganoff

Yield: 5 cups

Have ready:

1 pound frozen tofu, thawed, squeezed dry, and torn in bite-size pieces

Sauté together:

1 tablespoon olive oil
1 large onion, chopped
1 pound mushrooms, sliced
2 cloves garlic, minced

When the onions are almost transparent, add:

the tofu pieces

Stir and fry all together until the tofu starts to brown. Blend together, then stir in:

1 (12.3-ounce) package soft silken tofu
1 cup water
2 tablespoons soy sauce

Heat thoroughly and serve over rice or noodles.

Per Cup: Calories 171, Total Protein 12 g, Soy Protein 10 g,
Fat 9 g, Carbohydrates 10 g, Fiber 2 g, Calcium 213 mg, Sodium 419 mg

Broccoli-Mushroom Stir-Fry

Yield: 4 servings

Have ready:
  1 tablespoon minced fresh ginger
  1 cup sliced mushrooms
  Florets from 1½ pounds broccoli
  ½ pound regular or firm tofu, cut in small cubes
  2 tablespoons soy sauce
  ½ cup coarsely chopped walnuts

Heat in a wok:
  2 teaspoons oil
  1 teaspoon sesame oil

Add the ginger and stir-fry for 1 minute. Add the mushrooms and stir-fry for 3 minutes. Add the broccoli and stir-fry for about 6 minutes, then cover and steam until they are crisp-tender. Stir in the tofu, soy sauce, and walnuts; cook 1 more minute. Serve at once on rice or Chinese noodles.

Per Serving: Calories 206, Total Protein 8 g, Soy Protein 3 g,
Fat 13 g, Carbohydrates 12 g, Fiber 7 g, Calcium 161 mg, Sodium 553 mg

Chile Quiles

Yield: 6 servings

Serve with a green salad for a quick lunch or dinner.

Mix together:

1 pound regular tofu, mashed
1 cup picante sauce (your choice how hot)
1 teaspoon salt
¼ cup chopped fresh cilantro

Cut into quarters:

12 corn tortillas

Stir-fry the cut tortillas in a wok with:

1 tablespoon oil

When the tortillas start to get crisp, mix in the tofu mixture and continue to stir-fry until heated through.

Per Serving: Calories 221, Total Protein 10 g, Soy Protein 5 g,
Fat 7 g, Carbohydrates 28 g, Fiber 4 g, Calcium 239 mg, Sodium 763 mg

Baked Potatoes
with Chili Topping

Yield: 2 servings

Pick up baked potatoes at your local deli, or bake them at home.

Have ready:

2 medium baked potatoes
Heated *Chewy Chili*, p. 97

Make a cross cut on top of the potatoes, and squeeze to open. Pour the hot chili into the opening, and serve.

Per Serving: Calories 383, Total Protein 15 g, Soy Protein 6 g,
Fat 5 g, Carbohydrates 67 g, Fiber 9 g, Calcium 140 mg, Sodium 409 mg

Enchilada Casserole

Yield: 6 servings

Preheat the oven to 350°F.

Thaw, squeeze, and tear into bite-size pieces:

1 pound frozen tofu (you can substitute fresh regular tofu)

Have ready:

12 corn tortillas

to prepare the chile gravy, sauté until soft:

1 tablespoon olive oil
½ large onion, finely chopped

Mix together in a separate bowl:

3 tablespoons chile powder
3 tablespoons unbleached white flour
½ teaspoon garlic powder
½ teaspoon cumin
1 teaspoon salt

Add this to the soft onion, then whip in slowly without making lumps:

4 cups water

Bring to a boil.

Cover the bottom of an 11- x 17-inch or 9-x 9-inch pan with about half of the chile gravy. Lay on half of the tortillas, overlapping evenly. Cover with the tofu pieces, then more tortillas, and the rest of the chile gravy.

Sprinkle with:

½ cup grated dairy-free pepper Jack cheese
½ cup chopped black olives

Bake until bubbling, about 20 to 25 minutes.

Per Serving: Calories 266, Total Protein 12 g, Soy Protein 8 g,
Fat 10 g, Carbohydrates 30 g, Fiber 3 g, Calcium 327 mg, Sodium 524 mg

Tofu Alfredo

Yield: 4 to 6 servings

Cook in boiling water to al dente:

8 ounces linguine

Process in a blender or food processor:

2 cloves garlic
3 tablespoons dried basil, or ¾ ounce fresh basil leaves
3 tablespoons mellow white miso
1 (12.3-ounce) package firm silken tofu

Drain the pasta and toss with the sauce while still hot. Reheat if needed.

Per Serving: Calories 201, Total Protein 13 g, Soy Protein 7 g,
Fat 4 g, Carbohydrates 29 g, Fiber 2 g, Calcium 45 mg, Sodium 781 mg

Burritos Fritos

Yield: 8 burritos

Have ready:

2 (4-ounce) cans whole green chiles
8 ounces dairy-free cheddar or pepper Jack cheese, sliced
½ pound regular or firm tofu, cut into 8 sticks
8 large flour tortillas

Soften each tortilla on a hot griddle. Lay out one seeded green chile in the middle of each tortilla, top with one slice of cheese, then one tofu stick. Fold up like an envelope, then fry in hot oil until golden on both sides. Serve hot with salsa.

Per Burrito: Calories 227, Total Protein 14 g, Soy Protein 9 g,
Fat 8 g, Carbohydrates 25 g, Fiber 3 g, Calcium 265 mg, Sodium 441 mg

Lasagne

Yield: 6 servings

Preheat the oven to 350°F.

Cook in boiling water to al dente, then drain and rinse:

½ pound lasagne noodles

Have ready:

1 (26-ounce) jar your favorite low-sodium tomato-based pasta sauce

Sauté together:

1 tablespoon oil
1 medium onion, chopped
2 cloves garlic, minced

Blend in a food processor or blender until smooth and creamy:

1 pound regular tofu
¾ cup soy yogurt (optional)
1 teaspoon salt
¼ cup nutritional yeast flakes (optional)
½ cup chopped fresh basil
¼ cup chopped fresh parsley

Stir in the onion and garlic. Start making layers in a 2-quart baking dish, beginning with half of the tomato sauce on the bottom, then a layer using half of the noodles. Next, spread the tofu filling evenly over the noodles, arrange the other half of the noodles, and then pour over the rest of the tomato sauce.

This can be topped with:

½ cup grated dairy-free mozzarella and/or soy Parmesan

Bake for about 30 minutes, or until bubbling and the cheese is melted.

Per Serving: Calories 207, Total Protein 12 g, Soy Protein 8 g, Fat 7 g, Carbohydrates 22 g, Fiber 5 g, Calcium 255 mg, Sodium 477 mg

Lasagne Florentine

Yield: 6 servings

Preheat the oven to 350°F.

Cook in boiling water to al dente, then drain and rinse:
½ pound lasagne noodles

Have ready:
4 cups your favorite low-sodium tomato sauce

To make the tofu filling, mix together:
1 pound regular tofu, mashed or crumbled
1 (10-ounce) package frozen chopped spinach, thawed, or
1 pound fresh spinach, washed and chopped
1 tablespoon onion powder
1 teaspoon salt
½ teaspoon garlic powder
½ teaspoon basil

Start making layers in a 2-quart baking dish, beginning with half the tomato sauce on the bottom, then a layer of half the noodles, the tofu filling, the other half of the noodles, and the rest of the tomato sauce.

This can be topped with:
Grated dairy-free mozzarella and/or soy Parmesan (optional)

Bake for about 30 minutes or until bubbly.

Per Serving: Calories 174, Total Protein 11 g, Soy Protein 5 g,
Fat 4 g, Carbohydrates 23 g, Fiber 7 g, Calcium 257 mg, Sodium 449 mg

Lasagne
with Dairy-Free Cheese

Yield: 6 servings

Preheat the oven to 350°F.

Cook in boiling water to al dente, then rinse and drain:

½ pound lasagne noodles

Have ready:

4 cups your favorite low-sodium tomato sauce

To make the tofu filling, mix together:

1 pound regular tofu, mashed
1 tablespoon onion powder
6 ounces dairy-free mozzarella, grated
1 teaspoon salt
½ cup chopped fresh basil
¼ cup chopped fresh parsley
¼ teaspoon garlic powder

Start making layers in a 2-quart baking dish, beginning with half the tomato sauce on the bottom, then a layer of half the noodles, the tofu filling, the other half of the noodles, and the rest of the tomato sauce.

This can be topped with:

Soy Parmesan (optional)

Bake for about 30 minutes or until bubbly.

Per Serving: Calories 226, Total Protein 18 g, Soy Protein 12 g,
Fat 7 g, Carbohydrates 23 g, Fiber 7 g, Calcium 394 mg, Sodium 643 mg

Spring Rolls

Yield: 10 to 12 rolls

Have all the ingredients cut and ready before starting.

Cut into small 1- x ½- x ¼-inch pieces:

½ pound fresh regular or firm tofu or frozen tofu, thawed, and squeezed dry

Sprinkle over with:

1 tablespoon soy sauce

Set aside. In a wok or frying pan begin stir-frying:

1 tablespoon peanut oil
1 clove garlic, pressed
1½ tablespoons peeled and minced fresh ginger

Add and continue stir-frying for 1 minute:

2 green onions, cut into 1-inch pieces
1 cup fresh mushrooms, sliced
2 cups chopped greens (bok choy, Chinese cabbage, or other greens)
1 (4-ounce) can water chestnuts, drained and sliced
the tofu pieces

Stir, cover, and steam for 2 minutes, then add:

2 cups fresh mung bean sprouts

Stir in, then spoon about ⅓ cup into each:

Ready-made spring roll wrapper

Fold up and seal the edges with a dab of water on your finger. Fry in hot oil on both sides until browned. Spring rolls can also be oven-fried by placing the rolls on a well-oiled cookie sheet and brushing the tops with oil. Bake in a 400°F oven for 10 to 15 minutes on each side.

Per Roll: Calories 70, Total Protein 3 g, Soy Protein 2 g,
Fat 2 g, Carbohydrates 8 g, Fiber 1 g, Calcium 118 mg, Sodium 241 mg

Tamale Pie

Yield: 12 servings

Preheat the oven to 350°F.

Have ready:

1 pound frozen tofu, thawed, and squeezed dry, and torn into bite-size pieces

Sauté until transparent:

1 tablespoon oil
1 medium green pepper, chopped
1 medium onion, chopped
2 cloves garlic, minced

When almost tender, add:

the tofu pieces
2 tablespoons chile powder
½ teaspoon cumin
½ teaspoon salt
¼ teaspoon oregano

Stir and fry for a few minutes, then add:

1 (16-ounce) can diced tomatoes
1 (15-ounce) can tomato sauce
1 (10-ounce) package frozen cut corn
1 (6-ounce) can green chiles, chopped
½ cup whole small pitted black olives, drained

Mix well and pour into a 2½-quart casserole or a 9- x 13-inch baking dish. Cover the top with cornbread topping made from:

2 (8-ounce) packages corn muffin mix

Bake for about 25 minutes or until the cornbread is browned.

Per Serving: Calories 171, Total Protein 6 g, Soy Protein 3 g,
Fat 7 g, Carbohydrates 22 g, Fiber 5 g, Calcium 134 mg, Sodium 456 mg

Hawaiian Stir-Fry

Yield: 6 servings

Having everything ready on a tray before heating the wok or skillet makes stir-frying easy.

Have ready:

> 1 medium onion, cut into wedges
> 1 pound firm tofu, cut into ¾-inch cubes and sprinkled with
>   3 tablespoons soy sauce
> 1 green pepper, cut into 1-inch triangles
> 1 sweet red pepper, cut into 1-inch triangles
> 1 (5-ounce) can water chestnuts, sliced and drained
> 1 (15-ounce) can unsweetened pineapple chunks, drained,
>   reserving the juice

Stir together in a small saucepan:

> ¼ cup vinegar
> 2 tablespoons cornstarch

Stir in:

> ¼ cup sweetener of choice
> ½ cup vegetable stock
> the reserved pineapple juice

Cook and whisk over medium heat until clear and bubbly. Set aside.

Heat in a wok or skillet:

> 2 tablespoons oil

Stir in:

> 1 teaspoon minced fresh ginger

Stir in the onion wedges, cook for 2 minutes, add the tofu and cook for 1 more minute. Add the peppers and pineapple and stir. Add the chestnuts and sauce. Serve on rice with Chinese noodles.

Per Serving: Calories 227, Total Protein 7 g, Soy Protein 5 g,
Fat 7 g, Carbohydrates 32 g, Fiber 2 g, Calcium 175 mg, Sodium 514 mg

Noodles Romanoff

Yield: 8 servings

Preheat the oven to 350°F.

Boil in salted water until al dente, rinse, and drain:
1 pound flat noodles

Sauté together until transparent:
¼ cup olive oil
2 cloves garlic, minced
1 medium onion, chopped

Process in a blender or food processor until smooth and creamy:
1 (12.3-ounce) package soft or firm silken tofu
1 teaspoon salt

Combine all the ingredients, then fold in:
1 cup fresh chopped parsley (1½ ounces)
6 tablespoons soy Parmesan

Pour the mixture into a 2-quart baking dish, and bake for 15 to 20 minutes. Serve with more soy Parmesan. This can be made ahead and reheated later. It is also ready to eat without the baking, if you are in a big rush.

Per Serving: Calories 194, Total Protein 9 g, Soy Protein 5 g,
Fat 9 g, Carbohydrates 20 g, Fiber 1 g, Calcium 32 mg, Sodium 387 mg

Chewy Chili

Yield: 2 cups

This is a great dish for making at home or over a campfire.

Heat together in a saucepan until simmering:

1 (15-ounce) can vegetarian chili
½ cup water

Break up the tofu into small pieces and add to the simmering chili:

1 ounce snow-dried tofu

Simmer all together for another 5 minutes and serve.

Per Cup: Calories 238, Total Protein 13 g, Soy Protein 6 g,
Fat 5 g, Carbohydrates 33 g, Fiber 6 g, Calcium 132 mg, Sodium 401 mg

Angel Hair Primavera

Yield: 6 servings

Cook according to package directions:

12 ounces angel hair pasta or cappelini

Have ready:

1 pound zucchini, sliced
6 ounces mushrooms, cut in quarters (1½ cups)
6 ounces snow peas, trimmed (1½ cups)
2 cups your favorite tomato sauce, heated

Heat in a wok or skillet:

1 tablespoon olive oil

Add all the vegetables and stir-fry for about 5 minutes.

Add and toss in:

½ pound regular or firm tofu, cut into ½-inch cubes
Salt to taste

Serve on the angel hair pasta. Pass the tomato sauce and soy Parmesan.

Per Serving: Calories 172, Total Protein 7 g, Soy Protein 2 g,
Fat 4 g, Carbohydrates 26 g, Fiber 5 g, Calcium 110 mg, Sodium 462 mg

Oriental Stir-Fry

Yield: 5 servings

Have ready:
- **1 large onion, sliced**
- **2 ribs celery, sliced**
- **¼ pound snow peas, trimmed**
- **¼ pound fresh bean sprouts**
- **1 (8-ounce) can sliced water chestnuts, drained**
- **1 (6-ounce) can sliced mushrooms, or 1 cup fresh mushrooms**
- **6 small green onions, sliced with tops**
- **½ pound regular or firm tofu cut into ¾-inch cubes**

Heat in a wok or skillet:
- **1 tablespoon peanut oil**

Add the sliced onion and stir-fry for 2 minutes. Add the snow peas and fresh mushrooms if you are using them, and stir-fry for 2 more minutes. Stir in the water chestnuts, canned mushrooms if you are using them, sprouts, and green onions.

Next stir in the tofu and stir-fry another 2 minutes. Mix together and pour in:
- **¼ cup soy sauce**
- **1 teaspoon sweetener of choice**
- **¾ cup hot bouillon**

Stir-fry for 2 more minutes and serve over rice.

Per Serving: Calories 159, Total Protein 7 g, Soy Protein 4 g,
Fat 4 g, Carbohydrates 22 g, Fiber 5 g, Calcium 140 mg, Sodium 832 mg

Tofu Tacos

Yield: 2 cups filling (4 tacos)

See photo, page 104

Crumble into a bowl:

1 pound regular tofu

Sprinkle with:

1 (1.75-ounce) package taco seasoning mix

Mix this all together and brown in:

1 tablespoon olive oil

Serve in taco shells with the following fixings:

Chopped tomatoes
Lettuce
Onion
Grated dairy-free cheese (optional)
Hot sauce

For Tostadas: Bake or fry either corn or flour tortillas one at a time until crisp and golden. Drain on paper toweling. To build the tostada, start with the crisp tortilla, then the seasoned tofu, chopped tomatoes, green peppers, and lettuce, then top with optional grated cheese and chopped olives. Spoon on hot sauce to taste.

Per Taco: Calories 198, Total Protein 9 g, Soy Protein 8 g,
Fat 9 g, Carbohydrates 17 g, Fiber 1 g, Calcium 243 mg, Sodium 713 mg

Fajitas

Yield: 4 fajitas

This a colorful and tasty treat. See photo, page 103 and on the back cover.

Slice in thin strips:

1 pound frozen tofu, thawed and squeezed dry

Mix together and pour over the sliced tofu:

2 tablespoons soy sauce
2 tablespoons balsamic vinegar
2 cloves garlic, minced or pressed
2 tablespoons water

Press the slices so the liquid is absorbed evenly into the tofu.

Sauté together:

1 tablespoon olive oil
1 clove garlic
1 medium onion, sliced
1 red bell pepper, sliced
1 yellow bell pepper, sliced
1 green bell pepper, sliced
Hot pepper of choice, chopped (optional)

Remove and set aside, then add to the hot pan:

1 tablespoon olive oil
the tofu strips

Sauté until browned. Serve on heated flour tortillas with salsa on the side.

Per 1½ Cups Fajita Filling: Calories 179, Total Protein 10 g, Soy Protein 9 g, Fat 12 g, Carbohydrates 8 g, Fiber 2 g, Calcium 244 mg, Sodium 513 mg

Variation: Reconstitute 3 ounces snow-dried tofu in warm water for 5 minutes, then gently but firmly press the water out. Let the tofu soak up the marinade, slice thinly, and brown as directed above.

Curry

Yield: 6 servings

Thaw, squeeze out, and cut into bite-size pieces:

1 pound regular frozen tofu

Sauté until transparent:

1 tablespoon oil
1 large onion, cut in half moons
2 cloves garlic, pressed

Sprinkle over and stir in:

2 tablespoons unbleached white flour
1½ tablespoons curry powder
½ teaspoon freshly ground black pepper

Then stir in:

the bite-size pieces of tofu

Stir-fry for a few minutes until the tofu starts to brown, then stir in:

3 cups soymilk
1 teaspoon salt

Continue stirring until just before it comes to a boil, then turn off the heat. Serve on rice with any any combination of dairy-free yogurt, chutney, chopped peanuts, chopped cucumber, toasted coconut, and chopped green onions.

Per Serving: Calories 134, Total Protein 9 g, Soy Protein 8 g,
Fat 8 g, Carbohydrates 7 g, Fiber 2 g, Calcium 171 mg, Sodium 376 mg

Chinese Fried Rice with Tofu

Yield: 4 cups

Have ready:

½ pound regular or firm tofu, cut into small cubes
1 large onion, sliced
2 ribs celery, sliced
1 green pepper, sliced
2 cups cooked rice
2 green onions, with tops, cut in ½-inch pieces

Heat in a nonstick wok or skillet:

1 tablespoon oil

Add the tofu cubes, and stir-fry for 1 minute; stir in the soy sauce. Remove the tofu, and add to the wok:

1 tablespoon oil

Add the onion, celery, and green pepper, and stir-fry for 3 to 4 minutes. Crumble in the cooked rice, and stir-fry for 2 minutes.

Stir in the tofu plus:

1 tablespoon soy sauce

Serve topped with the green onions.

Per Cup: Calories 213, Total Protein 8 g, Soy Protein 4 g,
Fat 7 g, Carbohydrates 31 g, Fiber 3 g, Calcium 149 mg, Sodium 274 mg

Pictured to the right: Fajitas, page 100.

Pictured on page 104: Tofu Tacos, page 99

Deviled Tofu

Yield: 8 slices

Have ready:

1 pound tofu, cut into 8 slices
1½ cups fresh bread crumbs (can be made in the food processor
or blender from day-old bread)
2 tablespoons olive oil

Mix in a shallow dish:

½ cup Dijon mustard
½ cup green onions with tops, cut small
2 tablespoons soy sauce
1 teaspoon thyme
¼ teaspoon freshly ground black pepper

Dip the tofu slices into the mustard sauce, coating evenly, then into the bread crumbs, patting on the crumbs. Brown the coated tofu slices in a nonstick skillet, adding 1 tablespoon of the olive oil in the pan for each side.

Per Slice: Calories 123, Total Protein 5 g, Soy Protein 4 g,
Fat 8 g, Carbohydrates 5 g, Fiber 9 g, Calcium 130 mg, Sodium 719 mg

Pictured on page 105: top of the page Pesto Pizza, page 108, middle right Pizza with Tofu, page 108, bottom Southwestern Pizza, page 109.

Pictured to the left: first row from top left: Chocolate Truffle Pie, page, 121, Cheesecake, page, 118; second row Strawberries in Patty Shells, page, 131, Silky Chocolate Pudding, page, 127 Raspberry Pudding, page, 126, and Creamy Topping, page, 134 (in a glass).

On the glass serving dish in the large shells: clockwise from the top left edge of page: Silky Chocolate Pudding, page, 127, Apricot Pudding, page, 125 Creamy Cookie Pudding, page, 125, Chocolate Truffle Pie, page, 121 with Creamy Topping, page, 134, Raspberry Pudding, page, 126

Pizza with Tofu

Yield: 8 pieces

You can use pita breads for the crust to make individual pizzas. See photo, page 105.

Preheat the oven to 450°F.

Have ready:
1 (12-inch) ready-made pizza crust

Spread with:
1½ cups your favorite tomato sauce

Sprinkle over the top:
½ pound regular tofu, crumbled
1 cup sliced mushrooms
½ cup chopped green pepper
½ cup sliced olives
½ cup grated dairy-free mozzarella

Bake for about 15 minutes or until the cheese is melted.

Per Piece: Calories 140, Total Protein 7 g, Soy Protein 4 g,
Fat 5 g, Carbohydrates 17 g, Fiber 3 g, Calcium 143 mg, Sodium 511 mg

Pesto Pizza

Yield: 8 pieces

Try this savory, red and green pizza. See photo, page 105.

Have ready:
1 (12-inch) ready-made pizza crust
1½ cups *Pesto Dip or Spread*, p. 29

Preheat the oven to 450°F.

Spread the *Pesto Spread* evenly over the pizza crust, then top with:
4 to 6 roma tomatoes, sliced
1 to 2 banana peppers, sliced
¼ cup sliced or chopped red onion

Bake for about 8 to 10 minutes, and serve.

Per Piece: Calories 166, Total Protein 7 g, Soy Protein 3 g,
Fat 7 g, Carbohydrates 17 g, Fiber 3 g, Calcium 93 mg, Sodium 289 mg

Southwestern Pizza

Yield: 8 pieces

Here is a pizza with a different twist, the "cheese" goes on first. Use a round or oblong ready-made crust, and make it as spicy as you like.

Have ready:

1 (12-inch) fully baked thin pizza crust
4 ounces grated dairy-free pepper Jack cheese
½ pound *Fajita Strips*, p. 100, cut in bite-size pieces
¼ cup chopped red onion
½ cup corn kernels
¼ cup chopped green pepper
Jalapeño slices to taste
¼ cup salsa to taste

Preheat the oven to 450°F.

Spread the pepper Jack evenly over the crust, then sprinkle over the rest of the toppings. Bake for about 10 minutes or just until the pepper Jack melts.

Remove it from the oven, and sprinkle over the top:

⅓ cup chopped cilantro leaves

Per Piece: Calories 152, Total Protein 9 g, Soy Protein 6 g,
Fat 2 g, Carbohydrates 22 g, Fiber 2 g, Calcium 166 mg, Sodium 371 mg

Curried Basmati Rice
with Tofu & Peas

Yield: 5 cups

In a 2-quart saucepan, sauté until transparent:

2 tablespoons olive oil
1 large onion, chopped
2 cloves garlic

Stir in and cook for another minute:

1 to 2 tablespoons curry powder
½ teaspoon salt

Stir in:

1 cup basmati white or brown rice
1⅞ cups water
½ pound tofu, cut into ½-inch cubes

Bring to a boil, cover, and reduce the heat to simmer; cook for 20 minutes for white basmati rice, 45 minutes for brown, without stirring. Spread on top:

1 cup thawed frozen or fresh green peas

Cover and let stand for 10 minutes. Fluff all together with a fork, and serve.

Per Cup: Calories 214, Total Protein 7 g, Soy Protein 3 g,
Fat 7 g, Carbohydrates 29 g, Fiber 2 g, Calcium 119 mg, Sodium 219 mg

Golden Rice Pilaf

Yield: 5 cups

Sauté in a 2-quart saucepan until softened:

1 tablespoon oil
1 medium onion, chopped

Stir in and cook for 2 minutes to coat:

1 cup long grain rice

Add:

2½ cups hot vegetable bouillon
½ teaspoon coriander
½ cup raisins
½ teaspoon curry powder
½ teaspoon turmeric
½ teaspoon salt

Stir, cover, and cook over low heat for 10 to 12 minutes until most of the liquid is absorbed.

Remove from the heat and fluff into the rice:

½ pound regular or firm tofu, cut into ½-inch cubes

Cover and let sit for 10 minutes. Add and fluff in:

⅓ cup slivered, toasted almonds

Serve with a sprinkle of minced parsley.

Per ½ Cup: Calories 81, Total Protein 3 g, Soy Protein 1 g,
Fat 5 g, Carbohydrates 8 g, Fiber 1 g, Calcium 64 mg, Sodium 111 mg

Sloppy Joes

Yield: 3½ cups

Sauté together in a 10-inch skillet:

1 tablespoon olive oil
1 medium onion, diced
1 small green pepper

Mix together in a bowl:

1 pound regular tofu, crumbled
2 tablespoons soy sauce

Add the tofu mixture to the cooking onions and peppers, and continue cooking until the tofu starts to brown.

Stir in:

2 cups your favorite tomato sauce
1 tablespoon chili powder

Per ½ Cup: Calories 120, Total Protein 6 g, Soy Protein 5 g,
Fat 5 g, Carbohydrates 10 g, Fiber 2 g, Calcium 150 mg, Sodium 516 mg

For an even Quicker Sloppy Joe: Start by browning the tofu sprinkled with soy sauce in the olive oil, then add a 15-ounce can of prepared Sloppy Joe sauce, or a 1.5-ounce package dry flavoring mix for Sloppy Joe along with a 6-ounce can tomato paste and a cup of water.

Quick Garden Wraps

Yield: 4 wraps

This recipe makes use of ready-to-eat smoked tofu. There are other types of flavored tofu also available in the refrigerator section of your natural food store or grocery store. Have all the components cut and ready before you start wrapping. The following makes a nice combination, but you can change the ingredients according to taste or what you might have on hand. See photo, page 69.

On a hot griddle, heat:

4 (10-inch) flour or spinach tortilla wraps

Divide among the four tortillas and spread to within an inch of the edges of each:

**4 tablespoons dairy-free salad dressing
(such as soy mayonnaise)**

Divide among the tortillas, arranging evenly on top:

**1 (6-ounce) package smoked tofu, thinly sliced
4 ounces roasted red bell pepper, or thinly sliced fresh pepper
½ small avocado, thinly sliced
1½ cups grated carrot
1 medium tomato, thinly sliced
2 ounces arugula
4 to 6 ounces sprouts
Salsa or pesto to taste (optional)**

Roll up each tortilla, folding in the ends to keep the contents from escaping. Cut in half and enjoy.

*Per Wrap: Calories 275, Total Protein 9 g, Soy Protein 3 g,
Fat 11 g, Carbohydrates 32 g, Fiber 6 g, Calcium 112 mg, Sodium 324 mg*

Suggestion for other wrap fillings:

Sliced olives	**Sliced artichoke hearts**
Sliced onions	**Julienne jicama**
Roasted vegetables	**Shredded lettuce**
Sliced mushrooms	**Sliced hot peppers**
Different salad dressings	

Tofu Spanakopita

Yield: about 20 triangles

This classic Greek treat with a flaky phyllo wrap makes great finger food for appetizers, snacks, or a main dish. It takes a little time and planning ahead, but once you get the hang of it, it goes quickly and the end result is well worth it. Make sure your filling is ready to go before you open the thawed phyllo package, and take care to keep the phyllo leaves covered during the process so they don't dry out. Don't panic if your phyllo leaves crack or break, just put them in place and continue. A hand spray pump for the olive oil makes the process a little neater.

Have ready:

1 pound phyllo (fillo) leaves, thawed

1 pound fresh or frozen spinach, washed and chopped if fresh, thawed, drained, and squeezed dry if frozen

Sauté together:

1 tablespoon extra-virgin olive oil

1 large onion, chopped (about 2 cups)

2 cloves garlic, minced

When the onions are transparent, mix in:

1 pound regular tofu, crumbled or mashed

1 tablespoon fresh lemon juice

1 teaspoon salt

½ teaspoon freshly ground black pepper

½ teaspoon oregano or dill (optional)

Have ready:

¼ to ½ cup olive oil in a spray pump bottle or an oil brush

Preheat the oven to 375°F.

Have everything ready before opening the package of thawed phyllo leaves. (Read the package for directions.) Open the package and lay the stack of phyllo leaves flat on a towel. Cover with plastic wrap and keep the leaves covered this way as you continue with the process.

On a dry counter, fold one (14- x 18-inch) phyllo leaf in thirds vertically, making a 6- x 14-inch piece. (See drawing below.) Spray or brush the folded phyllo lightly and evenly with olive oil, then place ¼ cup of the filling at the bottom, shaping it into the form of a triangle, leaving about 1 inch of the phyllo at the bottom and sides. Turn the edges of the phyllo up over the filling about 1 inch from the bottom and in from both sides, covering the filling. Spray or brush the folded phyllo again with olive oil, then fold the lower right corner with the filling over at an angle to start the triangle shape. Continue to fold like a flag until the finished triangle is formed. Spray or brush again with olive oil over the entire folded triangle, and arrange on an oiled baking sheet. Bake for 15 to 20 minutes until browned and crisp. Serve hot.

Per triangle: Calories 124, Total Protein 4 g, Soy Protein 2 g,
Fat 5 g, Carbohydrates 17 g, Fiber 2 g, Calcium 84 mg, Sodium 209 mg

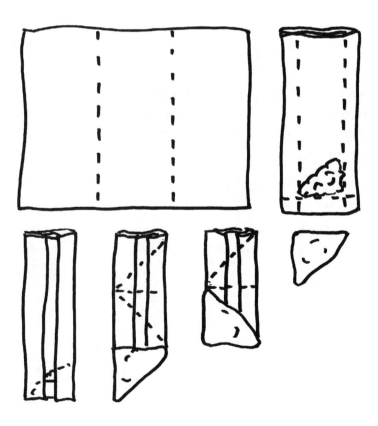

Baked Stuffed Potatoes

Yield: 4 servings

If you want to save some time, pick up already baked potatoes at your local deli or fast food market. This is also a great way to perk up leftover baked potatoes.

Preheat the oven to 400°F. Wash and pierce with a fork:

2 pounds baking potatoes

Bake for about 1 hour until tender and flaky.

While the potatoes are cooking, blend together:

¼ pound soft tofu
2 tablespoon nonhydrogenated margarine
2 teaspoons onion powder
½ teaspoon garlic powder
½ teaspoon salt
Freshly ground black pepper to taste

Take the potatoes out of the oven when they are done, and turn the oven temperature up to 450°F. Cut the potatoes in half lengthwise, and scoop out the fluffy insides into a bowl.

Mix the scooped-out potato with the blended mixture, using a potato masher or stiff wire whip, then stuff back into the potato skins. Sprinkle the tops with:

Soy Parmesan

Put the stuffed potatoes back in the oven for about 10 minutes until heated and slightly browned.

Per Serving: Calories 283, Total Protein 5 g, Soy Protein 2 g,
Fat 7 g, Carbohydrates 50 g, Fiber 4 g, Calcium 73 mg, Sodium 347 mg

DESSERTS

Almond Cheesecake ◆ 119

Apricot Pudding ◆ 125

Banana Bread ◆ 133

Cheesecake ◆ 118

Cherry Cobbler ◆ 124

Cherry Pudding ◆ 128

Chewy Brown Sugar Bars ◆ 122

Chocolate Truffle Pie ◆ 121

Creamy Chocolate Marble Pie ◆ 128

Creamy Cookie Pudding ◆ 125

Creamy Topping ◆ 134

Fresh Orange Pudding ◆ 126

Gingersnap-Lemon Ice Box Cake ◆ 129

Half & Half Cheesecake ◆ 120

Maple-Pecan Cheesecake ◆ 120

Pecan Pie ◆ 132

Pineapple Ice Box Cake ◆ 130

Raspberry Pudding ◆ 126

Silky Chocolate Pudding ◆ 127

Strawberries in Patty Shells
with Creamy Topping ◆ 131

Vanilla Rolled Cookies ◆ 123

Cheesecake

Yield: 1 (8-inch) cheesecake (12 servings)

This cheesecake is pictured on the front and back cover and page 106. Check the tips for blending tofu on pages 7 and 8.

Preheat the oven to 350°F.

Have ready:
   1 unbaked 8-inch graham cracker crust

Blend in a food processor or blender until smooth and creamy:
   1 pound regular or firm tofu
   1 cup sweetener of choice
   2 tablespoons fresh lemon juice
   1 tablespoon unbleached white flour
   1 teaspoon vanilla
   Pinch of salt

Pour into the unbaked pie shell, and bake for about 45 minutes, or until cracks start to form around the edge of the filling.

Top the cheesecake with *Creamy Topping*, page 134, and fresh fruit, or use any flavor fruit pie filling for a topping.

Per Serving: Calories 186, Total Protein 3 g, Soy Protein 3 g,
Fat 6 g, Carbohydrates 26 g, Fiber 1 g, Calcium 83 mg, Sodium 121 mg

Cherry or Blueberry Cheesecake: Fold 1 to 1½ cups pitted cherries or blueberries into the filling.

Variation: The cheesecake pictured on the cover was made in a spring-form pan. To make the cheesecake in a 9-inch springform pan, double the recipe. Crumble and press the graham cracker crust into the bottom of the pan. Pour the cheesecake filling over the crust, and bake for 50 to 60 minutes, or until cracks begin to appear around the edges. Cool and top with *Creamy Topping*, page 134, and fresh fruit.

Almond Cheesecake

Yield: 1 (8-inch) cheesecake (12 servings)

Check the tips on blending tofu on pages 7 and 8.

Have ready:

1 unbaked (8-inch) graham cracker crust

Chop in a food processor or blender:

1 cup toasted almonds

Add to the food processor or blender and process until smooth and creamy:

1 pound soft or regular tofu
¾ cup sweetener of choice
2 tablespoons fresh lemon juice
1 teaspoon almond extract
Pinch of salt

Pour into the unbaked pie shell, and bake for about 45 minutes, or until cracks start to form on the edge of the filling.

Per Serving: Calories 243, Total Protein 5 g, Soy Protein 3 g,
Fat 13 g, Carbohydrates 25 g, Fiber 2 g, Calcium 115 mg, Sodium 122 mg

Half & Half Cheesecake

Yield: 1 (8-inch) cheesecake (12 servings)

This makes an extra-creamy cheesecake.

Preheat the oven to 350°F.

Have ready:
1 unbaked (8-inch) graham cracker crust

Blend in a food processor or blender until smooth and creamy:
½ pound regular or firm tofu
8 ounces dairy-free cream cheese
1 cup sweetener of choice
2 tablespoons fresh lemon juice
1 teaspoon vanilla
Pinch of salt

Pour into the pie shell, and bake for about 45 minutes.

Per Serving: Calories 209, Total Protein 3 g, Soy Protein 1 g,
Fat 10 g, Carbohydrates 27 g, Fiber 1 g, Calcium 44 mg, Sodium 200 mg

Maple-Pecan Cheesecake

Yield: 1 (8-inch) cheesecake (12 servings)

Check the tips for blending tofu on pages 7 and 8.

Preheat the oven to 350°F.

Have ready:
1 (8-inch) unbaked graham cracker crust

Blend in a food processor or blender until smooth and creamy:
1 pound regular or firm tofu
1 cup maple syrup
Pinch of salt

Fold in:
½ cup broken pecan pieces

Pour into the pie shell, and bake for about 45 minutes or until cracks start to appear around the edge of the filling. Serve cold, topped with maple syrup and pecans or *Creamy Topping*, page 134.

Per Serving: Calories 221, Total Protein 4 g, Soy Protein 3 g,
Fat 10 g, Carbohydrates 20 g, Fiber 1 g, Calcium 110 mg, Sodium 124 mg

Chocolate Truffle Pie

Yield: 1 (8-inch) pie (12 servings)

This rich and creamy, crowd-pleasing dessert can be made a day ahead and chilled overnight for the best results, or can be frozen for a truly chilly treat that can be made several days ahead. Check the tips for blending tofu on pages 7 and 8. See photo, page 106.

Have ready:

1 (8-inch) graham cracker crust, baked

Blend in a food processor or blender until creamy:

1 pound firm or extra-firm tofu
⅔ cup granulated sweetener of choice
1 teaspoon vanilla, almond, coffee, or mint extract

Melt over hot water or in a microwave until they just start to melt:

6 ounces chocolate chips

Stir the melting chips together until they are all melted and creamy. Add to the mixture in the food processor or blender, and process immediately until smooth and creamy.

Pour and spread the mixture into the baked crust, and smooth with a spatula or shake carefully to fit into the shell. Chill for at least 4 hours or overnight until firm and sliceable.

Per Serving: Calories 234, Total Protein 4 g, Soy Protein 3 g,
Fat 12 g, Carbohydrates 28 g, Fiber 1 g, Calcium 86 mg, Sodium 123 mg

Variation: For an even richer and firmer pie, use up to 12 ounces chocolate chips.

Chewy Brown Sugar Bars

Yield: 24 bars

Preheat the oven to 350°F.

Combine in a mixing bowl:

2 cups unbleached white flour
1½ teaspoons baking powder
½ teaspoon salt

Process in a blender until the seeds are chopped and it becomes thick:

2 tablespoons flaxseed
½ cup warm water

Add to the blender:

½ pound regular tofu, crumbled
1 cup brown sugar or other granulated sweetener
½ cup oil
1 teaspoon vanilla

Pour this into the dry ingredients and beat until smooth. Fold in:

1 cup semi-sweet chocolate chips
½ cup chopped walnuts (optional)

Pour and spread into a 9- x 13-inch baking pan or two 8-inch round pans, and bake for about 25 minutes until browned and the bars bounce back to the touch of a finger in the middle.

Per Bar: Calories 143, Total Protein 2 g, Soy Protein 1 g,
Fat 8 g, Carbohydrates 17 g, Fiber 2 g, Calcium 30 mg, Sodium 49 mg

Vanilla Rolled Cookies

Yield: about 30 (3-inch) cookies

Preheat the oven to 350°F.

Cream together in a food processor:
   ¾ cup brown granulated sweetener
   ½ cup nonhydrogenated margarine
   ½ pound soft tofu
   2 teaspoons vanilla

Mix together in a bowl:
   3 cups unbleached white flour
   2 teaspoons baking powder
   ½ teaspoon salt

Add the dry ingredients to the wet, and pulse only until blended (about 10 pulses).

Roll out ¼ inch thick, and cut into shapes. Bake for 8 to 10 minutes.

Per Cookie: Calories 86, Total Protein 2 g, Soy Protein 1 g,
Fat 3 g, Carbohydrates 12 g, Fiber 0 g, Calcium 40 mg, Sodium 73 mg

Cherry Cobbler

Yield: 9 servings

Preheat the oven to 375°F.

Blend together in a food processor:

1 cup flour
1 teaspoon baking powder

Add while the processor is running:

¼ pound soft tofu
2 tablespoons oil
½ cup soymilk
⅓ cup sweetener of choice

Process only until the dough is just blended, then spread it in an oiled 8- x 8-inch pan.

Cover with:

1 (17-ounce) can pitted sweetened dark cherries, drained with juice reserved

Heat the reserved cherry juice to a boil, and pour over all. Bake for 40 to 45 minutes, and serve warm.

Per Serving: Calories 136, Total Protein 3 g, Soy Protein 1 g,
Fat 3 g, Carbohydrates 23 g, Fiber 1 g, Calcium 54 mg, Sodium 3 mg

Creamy Cookie Pudding

Yield: 2¼ cups (4 servings)

Tofu makes luscious puddings and pie fillings. The silken tofu in aseptic packaging produces a soft texture with a shiny appearance. Traditional tofu yields a more dense, creamy texture. Take advantage of the variety of ready-made pie and small tart shells available on the grocery shelves or in the freezer. Some are already cooked and just need to be filled. See photo, page 106.

Blend in a food processor or blender until smooth and creamy:

1 (12.3-ounce) package low-fat, firm silken tofu
½ cup granulated sweetener of choice
1 teaspoon vanilla
Pinch of salt

Break into quarters or smaller pieces, and fold in:

10 chocolate sandwich cookies with vanilla filling

Pour or spoon into individual serving dishes, and chill until set.

Per Serving: Calories 259, Total Protein 8 g, Soy Protein 6 g,
Fat 6 g, Carbohydrates 41 g, Fiber 0 g, Calcium 0 mg, Sodium 199 mg

Apricot Pudding

Yield: 1¾ cups (3 servings)

See photo, page 106.

Blend together in a food processor or blender:

½ pound regular tofu
¼ cup sweetener of choice

Add and blend in:

1 (20-ounce) can apricot halves, drained (you can reserve a few halves for garnish)

Pour into serving dishes, chill, and serve.

Per Serving: Calories 194, Total Protein 6 g, Soy Protein 5 g,
Fat 3 g, Carbohydrates 35 g, Fiber 3 g, Calcium 152 mg, Sodium 21 mg

Raspberry Pudding

Yield: 1½ cups

See photo, page 106.

Blend in a food processor or blender until smooth and creamy:

**5 ounces frozen raspberries (you can reserve a few whole
berries for garnish)**
½ pound firm tofu
¼ cup sweetener of choice
Pinch of salt

Pour into serving dishes and chill.

*Per ½ Cup: Calories 166, Total Protein 6 g, Soy Protein 5 g,
Fat 3 g, Carbohydrates 28 g, Fiber 2 g, Calcium 160 mg, Sodium 6 mg*

Fresh Orange Pudding

Yield: about 4 cups

Have ready:

2 navel oranges, cut in bite-size pieces

Blend in a food processor or blender until smooth and creamy:

½ pound regular tofu
¼ cup sweetener of choice
1 teaspoon vanilla
Pinch of salt

Fold the orange pieces in, and serve at once.

*Per ½ Cup: Calories 60, Total Protein 2 g, Soy Protein 2 g,
Fat 1 g, Carbohydrates 10 g, Fiber 1 g, Calcium 71 mg, Sodium 4 mg*

Fresh Fruit Pudding: Substitute any fresh fruit cut in bite-size pieces for
the navel oranges.

Fruit Cocktail Pudding: Substitute 2 cups drained fruit cocktail for the
navel oranges.

Silky Chocolate Pudding

Yield: 1¾ cups (3 servings)

This is a low-fat, creamy, dark chocolate pudding. Regular tofu makes a thick, creamy pudding. Use silken tofu for a shiny, soft, creamy pudding. See photo, page 106.

Blend together in a food processor or blender until smooth and creamy:

1 (12.3-ounce) package low-fat, firm silken tofu, or
    ¾ pound regular tofu
½ cup granulated sweetener of choice
¼ cup cocoa
1 teaspoon vanilla
Pinch of salt

Pour into serving dishes and chill.

Per Serving: Calories 198, Total Protein 10 g, Soy Protein 8 g,
Fat 2 g, Carbohydrates 35 g, Fiber 3 g, Calcium 10 mg, Sodium 112 mg

Cherry Pudding

Yield: 2 cups

Blend in a food processor or blender until smooth and creamy:

½ pound regular tofu
½ pound fresh or frozen dark sweet pitted cherries
¼ cup sweetener of choice
Pinch of salt

Pour into serving dishes and chill.

Per ½ Cup: Calories 43, Total Protein 4 g, Soy Protein 4 g,
Fat 2 g, Carbohydrates 1 g, Fiber 0 g, Calcium 114 mg, Sodium 4 mg

Creamy Chocolate Marble Pie

Yield: 1 (8-inch) pie (8 servings)

Have ready:

1 (8-inch) graham cracker crust, baked

Blend together in a food processor or blender until smooth and creamy:

1 pound regular tofu
⅔ cup sweetener of choice
2 teaspoons vanilla
Pinch of salt

Spread all but 1 cup of this mixture in the baked pie shell.

Add to the 1 cup left in the food processor or blender:

3 tablespoons cocoa

Process until mixed in, then drop spoonfuls of the chocolate into the vanilla. Swirl the two together with a knife, and chill until firm.

Per Serving: Calories 252, Total Protein 6 g, Soy Protein 4 g,
Fat 11 g, Carbohydrates 32 g, Fiber 1 g, Calcium 125 mg, Sodium 182 mg

Gingersnap-Lemon Ice Box Cake

Yield: 9 servings

Have ready:

1½ cups *Creamy Topping*, p. 134

Cover the bottom of an 8- x 8-inch cake pan with:

14 gingersnaps, broken into crumbs

Spread over these:

1 (20-ounce) can lemon pie filling

Cover with the *Creamy Topping*, then sprinkle with:

12 gingersnaps, crushed

Refrigerate at least 4 hours or overnight until firm.

Per Serving: Calories 141, Total Protein 3 g, Soy Protein 3 g,
Fat 3 g, Carbohydrates 26 g, Fiber 1 g, Calcium 11 mg, Sodium 160 mg

Pineapple Ice Box Cake

Yield: 9 servings

Crush in a paper bag or food processor:

1 (10-ounce) package sugar wafer cookies

Reserve half the crumbs for topping, and sprinkle half on the bottom of a 9- x 9-inch pan.

Have ready:

1 (20-ounce) can crushed pineapple, reserving the juice

Blend in a food processor or blender until smooth and creamy:

1 pound regular tofu
½ cup sweetener of choice
¼ cup lemon juice
The reserved pineapple juice

Pour onto the crumbs, top with the crushed pineapple, and sprinkle the reserved crumbs over the top. Chill at least 4 hours or overnight until firm.

Per Serving: Calories 285, Total Protein 5 g, Soy Protein 4 g,
Fat 10 g, Carbohydrates 43 g, Fiber 1 g, Calcium 111 mg, Sodium 44 mg

Strawberries in Patty Shells
with Creamy Topping

Yield: 6 servings

This is a quick and easy dessert that is perfect for strawberry season, but also works well with frozen berries. See photo, page 106.

Bake according to package directions:

6 frozen patty shells

While they are baking, prepare:

1½ cups *Creamy Topping*, p. 134

Wash and trim:

2 pints strawberries

Stir into the berries:

½ cup sweetener of choice

Fill each cooled patty shell with *Creamy Topping*, then spoon strawberries over the top.

Per Serving: Calories 375, Total Protein 6 g, Soy Protein 4 g, Fat 16 g, Carbohydrates 49 g, Fiber 4 g, Calcium 33 mg, Sodium 246 mg

Pecan Pie

Yield: 1 (8-inch) pie (12 servings)

Try this for a holiday pie.

Preheat the oven to 350°F.

Have ready:

1 (8-inch) unbaked pie crust

Blend in a food processor or blender until smooth and creamy:

½ pound regular tofu
1 cup brown granulated sweetener of choice
1 teaspoon vanilla
⅓ cup light molasses
¼ teaspoon salt

Fold in:

1½ cups whole pecan pieces

Pour into the unbaked pie shell, and bake for about 45 minutes or until cracks start to form around the edge of the filling. Serve with *Creamy Topping*, p 134, or vanilla soy ice cream.

Per Serving: Calories 280, Total Protein 3 g, Soy Protein 1 g,
Fat 14 g, Carbohydrates 34 g, Fiber 1 g, Calcium 70 mg, Sodium 157* mg

Banana Bread

Yield: 1 loaf (9 servings)

Make use of those ripe bananas and leftover tofu for a sweet treat.

Preheat the oven to 350°F.

Blend or beat in a food processor or mixing bowl:

2 ripe bananas
¼ pound soft tofu

Add and beat or process in until smooth:

½ cup granulated sweetener of choice
1 teaspoon vanilla

In another bowl, mix together:

1 cup whole wheat flour
1 cup unbleached flour
½ teaspoon baking powder
½ teaspoon baking soda
¼ teaspoon salt

Add the mixture to the wet ingredients, and beat or process just until smooth. Fold in:

½ cup chopped walnuts

Spread the batter into a loaf pan. Bake for 30 to 35 minutes until brown. Let cool for about 15 minutes before removing from the pan.

*Per Serving: Calories 205, Total Protein 5 g, Soy Protein 1 g,
Fat 5 g, Carbohydrates 35 g, Fiber 3 g, Calcium 58 mg, Sodium 62 mg*

Creamy Topping

Here are two different ways to make a no-cholesterol, low-fat, sweet and creamy topping for desserts.

Yield: 1½ cups

Process in a blender or food processor until smooth and creamy:

1 (12.3-ounce) package firm silken tofu
⅓ cup sweetener of choice
1½ teaspoons vanilla
1 teaspoon lemon juice
⅛ teaspoon salt

Per 2 tablespoons: Calories 38, Total Protein 2 g, Soy Protein 2 g,
Fat 1 g, Carbohydrates 6 g, Fiber 0 g, Calcium 8 mg, Sodium 33 mg

Yield: 1 cup

Process in a blender or food processor until smooth and creamy:

½ pound regular tofu
¼ cup sweetener of choice
1 teaspoon vanilla
½ teaspoon lemon juice
⅛ teaspoon salt

Per 2 tablespoons: Calories 44, Total Protein 2 g, Soy Protein 2 g,
Fat 1 g, Carbohydrates 7 g, Fiber 0 g, Calcium 57 mg, Sodium 37 mg

Index

A

Alfredo 89
almonds
  Amandine Tofu 82
  Cheesecake 119
  Rice Pilaf 111
  Roasted Pepper-Zucchini
    Salad 47
Angel Hair Primavera 97
antioxidants 5
apples
  Kuchen 13
  Waldorf Salad 36
  Whole Grain Pancakes 12
Apricot Pudding 125
artichoke hearts
  Pasta-Tofu Salad 45
asparagus
  Pasta-Tofu Salad 45
avocado
  -Cucumber Soup 65
  Salad 35
  Salad, Stuffed 41
  Taco Salad 32

B

Baked Potatoes 87
Balls, Spaghetti 75
Banana Bread 133
Barbecue Tofu 78
Bars, Brown Sugar 122
basil
  Bruchettas 20
  -Garlic Dressing 51
  Pesto Dip or Spread 29
  Stuffed Shells 83
Beet Salad, Roasted 49
bell peppers
  Corn Chowder 60
  Fajitas 100
  Garden Wraps 113
  Hawaiian Stir-Fry 95
  Roasted Pepper-Zucchini
    Salad 47
  Sweet Pepper-Tofu Salad 43
blending tofu 7, 8
Blueberry Cheesecake 118
Boofers 17
Bread, Banana, 133
bread crumbs
  breading mixes 76
  Deviled Tofu 107
Broccoli-Mushroom Stir-Fry 86
Broccoli Quiche 18
Brown Sugar Bars 122

Bruchettas 20
Burgers 75
Burritos Fritos 89

C

cabbage
  Miso Vegetable Soup 62
  Pineapple-Peanut Slaw 36
  Spring Rolls 93
  -Tofu Stir-Fry 84
Cashew Spread 25
celery
  Chinese Fried Rice 102
  Corn Chowder 60
  Mock Chicken Salad 39
  Oriental Stir-Fry 98
  Potato Salad 46
  Spinach-Pine Nut Salad 37
Cheesecake 118-20
cheeses, dairy-free 10
  Burritos Fritos 89
  Enchilada Casserole 88
  Lasagne 90
  Pizza 108
  Southwestern Pizza 109
  Stuffed Shells 83
Cherry Cheesecake 118
Cherry Cobbler 124
Cherry Pudding 128
chick-peas. See *garbanzo beans*
Chicken Salad, Mock 39
Chile Quiles 87
chiles
  Burritos Fritos 89
  Mexicali Rice Bake 22
  Tamale Pie 94
  Tofu Rancheros 16
Chili 61
Chili, Chewy 97
Chili-Style Breading Mix 77
Chili Topping 87
Chinese Fried Rice 102
Chocolate Marble Pie 128
Chocolate Pudding 127
Chocolate Truffle Pie 121
Chowder, Corn 60
Chutney Dressing 51
cilantro
  Garbanzo Bean Salad 40
  Southwestern Pizza 109
Cobbler, Cherry 124
Cole Slaw Dressing 55
Cookie Pudding 125
cookies and bars
  Brown Sugar Bars 122
  Vanilla Rolled Cookies 123
corn
  Chowder 60
  Southwestern Pizza 109
  Tamale Pie 94

cream cheese, dairy-free
  Half & Half Cheesecake 120
Creamy Salad Dressing 53
Cruise Ship Mustard Dressing
  56
cucumbers
  -Avocado Soup 65
  -Dill Dip 28
  -Dill Dressing 55
  -Dill Salad 42
  Gazpacho 64
Curried Basmati Rice 110
Curried Rice Salad 41
Curried Spinach Dip 30
Curry 101
Curry-Chutney Dip 26
Curry Dressing 54

D-E

Deviled Tofu 107
dill
  -Cucumber Dip 28
  -Cucumber Dressing 55
  -Cucumber Salad 42
dips 24-30
dressings, salad 51-56
Enchilada Casserole 88

F

Fajitas 100
Far East Dip 25
Four Bean Salad 48
freezing tofu 7
Fried Rice 21
Fried Tofu 74
Fried Tofu, Oven- 76-77
Fruit Salad Dressing 53

G

garbanzo beans
  Four Bean Salad 48
  Garbanzo Bean Salad 40
Garden Wraps 113
Garlic Lo-Cal Dressing 54
Garlic-Basil Dressing 51
Gazpacho 64
Gingersnap-Lemon Ice Box
  Cake 129
green beans
  Four Bean Salad 48
Green Dip or Spread 24
Green Goddess Dip 30
Green Rice 81
Gumbo Soup 58

H-I-J-K

Half & Half Cheesecake 120
Hash Browns 17
Hawaiian Stir-Fry 95
Herb Dip 29
Horseradish Dip 24

Hot Pink Dip 24
Iowa Potato Salad 46
isoflavones 5
Italian-Style Breading Mix 77
kidney beans
   Chili 61
   Four Bean Salad 48

L
Lasagne 90
Lasagne Florentine 91
Lasagne with Dairy-Free Cheese 92
Lebanese Salad 38
Lemon-Gingersnap Ice Box Cake 129
Lentil Soup 71
Loaf 75

M
macaroni
   and Tofu 80
   Seashell Salad 44
mango chutney
   Curried Rice Salad 41
   Curry-Chutney Dip 26
Maple-Pecan Cheesecake 120
marinating tofu 8
measuring tofu 7-8
Mexicali Rice Bake 22
miso
   Cole Slaw Dressing 55
   Cucumber-Avocado Soup 65
   Curried Spinach Dip 30
   Dip 28
   Vegetable Soup 62
Mock Chicken Salad 39
Mock Sour Cream Dressing 52
mushrooms
   Angel Hair Primavera 97
   -Broccoli Stir-Fry 86
   -Onion Breading Mix 76
   Oriental Stir-Fry 98
   Pizza 108-09
   Quiche 19
   Scrambled Tofu 15
   Spring Rolls 93
   Stroganoff 85
Mustard Dressing, Cruise Ship 56

N
nondairy cheeses 9. See also
   cheeses, dairy-free
nonhydrogenated margarine 10
noodles
   Pasta-Tofu Salad 45

(noodles, cont.)
   Roasted Pepper-Zucchini Salad 47
   Romanoff 96
   Soup, Ramen 63
nutritional yeast 9-10

O
olives
   -Pecan Spread 27
   Southwestern Pizza 109
Onion-Mushroom Breading Mix 76
Onion Soup Dip 26
Onion-Tomato Breading Mix 77
onions
   Fried Rice 21
Orange Pudding 126
Orange Tofu 79
Oriental Stir-Fry 98
Oven-Fried Tofu 76-77

P
Pancakes, Whole Grain 12
Parmesan, soy
   Noodles Romanoff 96
parsley
   Green Goddess Dip 30
   Noodles Romanoff 96
pasta
   Angel Hair Primavera 97
   Macaroni and Tofu 80
   Noodles Romanoff 96
   Roasted Pepper-Zucchini Salad 47
   Seashell Salad 44
   Stuffed Shells 83
   Tofu Alfredo 89
   -Tofu Salad 45
Peanut-Pineapple Slaw 36
peas
   Curried Basmati Rice 110
   Garbanzo Bean Salad 40
pecans
   Maple-Pecan Cheesecake 120
   -Olive Spread 27
   Pie 132
Pesto Dip or Spread 29
Pesto Pizza 108
phyllo
   Spanakopita 114-15
phytochemicals 5
pickle relish
   Tartar Sauce 27
   Tofu Salad 43
pies
   Chocolate Marble 128

(pies, cont.)
   Chocolate Truffle 121
   Pecan 132
pine nuts
   Pesto Dip or Spread 29
   Spinach Salad 37
pineapple
   Hawaiian Stir-Fry 95
   Ice Box Cake 130
   -Peanut Slaw 36
Pink Lo-Cal Dressing 54
pinto beans
   Chili 61
   Salad 37
Pizza 108-09
potatoes
   Baked 87
   Baked Stuffed 116
   Boofers 17
   Corn Chowder 60
   Hash Browns 17
   Potato Tofu Soup 72
   Pumpkin Soup 71
   Salad 46
   Spinach Soup 66
Primavera, Angel Hair 97
puddings
   Apricot 125
   Cherry 128
   Chocolate 127
   Creamy Cookie 125
   Orange 126
   Raspberry 126
Pumpkin Soup 71

Q-R
Quiche, Broccoli 18
Quiche, Mushroom 19
quick breads
   Banana Bread 133
radishes
   Pinto Bean Salad 37
raisins
   Rice Pilaf 111
Ramen Noodle Soup 63
Rancheros, Scrambled Tofu 16
Raspberry Pudding 126
rice
   Chinese Fried 102
   Curried Basmati 110
   Fried 21
   Green 81
   Mexicali Bake 22
   Pilaf, Golden 111
   Salad, Curried 41
   Spanish 22
Roasted Pepper-Zucchini Salad 47
Rolled Cookies, Vanilla 123

S

salad dressings 51-56
salads 37-50
Sauce, Tartar 27
Scrambled Tofu 14
  Rancheros 16
  Mushroom 15
Seashell Salad 44
sesame seeds
  Cabbage-Tofu Stir-Fry 84
  Spinach Salad 50
Shells, Stuffed 83
silken tofu 6. See also *tofu, silken*
  measuring 8
Slaw, Pineapple-Peanut 36
Sloppy Joes 112
smoked tofu
  Garden Wraps 113
snow peas
  Angel Hair Primavera 97
  Oriental Stir-Fry 98
Sour Cream Dressing, Mock 52
sour tofu 6
Southwestern Pizza 109
soy protein and disease 5
soy yogurt
  Mock Sour Cream Dressing
    52
soymilk
  Curry 101
  Macaroni and Tofu 80
  Spinach Soup 66
  Whole Grain Pancakes 12
Spanakopita 114-15
Spanish Rice 22
spinach
  Curried Spinach Dip 30
  Green Dip or Spread 24
  Green Rice 81
  Lasagne Florentine 91
  Lebanese Salad 38
  Miso Vegetable Soup 62
  -Pine Nut Salad 37
  Sesame Spinach Salad 50
  Soup 66
  Spanakopita 114-15
Spring Rolls 93
Stir-Fry, Hawaiian 95
Stir-Fry, Oriental 98
storing tofu 6-7
Strawberries in Patty Shells 131
Stroganoff 85
Stuffed Shells 83
Sweet Pepper-Tofu Salad 43

T

Taco Salad 32
Tacos 99
Tamale Pie 94
Tartar Sauce 27
tofu
  blending 7, 8
  marinating 8
  nutritional content of 4-5
  regular 5-6
  purchasing 6
  storing 6-7
tofu, frozen 7
  Barbecue Tofu, 78
  Curry, 101
  Enchilada Casserole, 88
  Fajitas, 100
  Gumbo Soup, 58
  Ramen Noodle Soup, 63
  Southwestern Chili, 60
  Stroganoff, 85
  Tamale Pie, 94
Tofu Salad 43
tofu, silken 6
  Alfredo 89
  Basil-Garlic Dressing 51
  Chocolate Pudding 127
  Cole Slaw Dressing 55
  Cool Cucumber-Avocado
    Soup 65
  Creamy Cookie Pudding 125
  Cruise Ship Mustard Dressing
    56
  Curry Dressing 54
  Fruit Salad Dressing 53
  Garlic Lo-Cal Dressing 54
  Green Rice 81
  Iowa Potato Salad 46
  Mock Sour Dream Dressing
    52
  Potato Tofu Soup 72
  Stroganoff 85
tofu, smoked
  Garden Wraps 113
tofu, snow-dried 6
  Baked Potatoes with Chili
    Topping, 87
  Chewy Chili, 97
  Fajitas, 100
tomato sauce
  Angel Hair Primavera 97
  Lasagne 90
  Lasagne Florentine 91
  Lasagne with Dairy-Free
    Cheese 92
  Pizza 108

(tomato sauce, cont.)
  Sloppy Joes 112
  Southwestern Pizza 109
Tomato-Onion Breading Mix 77
Tomato-Onion Soup Dip 26
tomatoes
  Avocado Salad 35
  Bruchettas 20
  Gazpacho 64
  Gumbo Soup 58
  Hot Pink Dip 24
  Lebanese Salad 38
  Scrambled Tofu Rancheros 16
  Taco Salad 32
  Tamale Pie 94
Topping, Creamy 134
tortillas
  Burritos Fritos 89
  Chile Quiles 87
  Enchilada Casserole 88
  Garden Wraps 113
Tostadas 99

V

Vanilla Rolled Cookies 123
Vegetable Soup, Miso 62
Vegetable Tofu Soup, Quick 59
vegetables, mixed
  Gumbo Soup 58
  Ramen Noodle Soup 63
Vegetarian Support Formula,
  Red Star 9-10
vitamin B12 9

W-Z

Waldorf Salad 36
walnuts
  Apple Kuchen 13
  Banana Bread 133
  Broccoli-Mushroom Stir-Fry
    86
  Far East Dip 25
  Pesto Dip or Spread 29
  Waldorf Salad 36
Whole Grain Pancakes 12
Wraps, Garden 113
zucchini
  Angel Hair Primavera 97
  Roasted Pepper Salad 47

More books from Louise Hagler

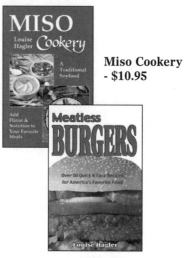

**Miso Cookery
- $10.95**

**Tofu Cookery
- $16.95**

**Meatless Burgers
- $9.95**

Tofu Quick & Easy - $11.95

**New Farm Vegetarian
Cookbook - $9.95**

**Soyfoods Cookery
- $9.95**

**Lighten Up!
with Louise Hagler
- $16.95**

Purchase these vegetarian cookbooks from your local bookstore or natural foods store, or you can buy them directly from:

Book Publishing Company

P.O. Box 99

Summertown, TN 38483

1-800-695-2241

Please include $3.50 per book for shipping and handling.

To find your favorite vegetarian and soyfood products online, visit:

www.healthy-eating.com